THE CHALLENGE OF MISSIONS

THE CHALLENGE
OF MISSIONS

BY

OSWALD J. SMITH, Litt.D.
Founder of The People's Church, Toronto

Foreword by
MARK BRAZEE
Eternal Word Ministries

MBM Publications

First published by Marshall Pickering, part of the HarperCollins
Publishing Group

ISBN (UK): 1 89935301 1
ISBN (USA): 0-934445-08-7

MBM Publications
Broken Arrow, Oklahoma

CONTENTS

FOREWORD

Over the past twenty-five years I have come across many books in the realm of Christian publications that have ministered to me. Through the writings of many men and women of God, I have been encouraged, challenged, and had great vision imparted to my life.

However, seldom have I encountered writings that have been able to take the stirrings of my heart, and the very foundation of the vision that God has placed in my spirit, and translate them into understandable and applicable words as much as Oswald J. Smith's book, *The Challenge of Missions*.

As I was walking through a used Christian bookstore searching for 'hidden treasures', I stumbled across this book. Being somewhat familiar with Rev. Smith's writings, I decided to purchase the book. When I started reading it, I couldn't put it down. His zeal for the world, his understanding of prosperity and its highest purpose, his perception of the apostle Paul's missionary methods, and his first-hand knowledge of how a local church with God's heart and vision can touch the world are all truths that Oswald J. Smith proved out many years ago, and will still bear fruit today. The messages in this book not only stirred me, but also stretched my thinking, enlarged my vision, and put a fire in me to do more, send more, and go more than I ever have before.

As you read the pages of this book, don't simply read the *words*, but listen to the heart of the man—and to what the Spirit is saying to the Church of the last days. As you read, I pray you will not only be challenged, but consumed by the mission of the Church . . . *Missions*. May you either go, or send a substitute.

Mark Brazee
Eternal Word Ministries
Broken Arrow, Oklahoma

CHAPTER I

SATAN'S DEFEAT

"WELL, what news?" inquired Satan, looking up with an expression of inquiry on his face.

"Great! the very best!" responded the Prince of Alaska, who had just entered.

"Have any of the Eskimos heard yet?" questioned the eager leader, his eyes fastened on the fallen angel.

"Not one!" answered the Prince, bowing low. "No, indeed, not a single individual. I have seen to that," he continued, as though gloating over a recent victory.

"Any attempts?" questioned his lord in a tone of authority. "Have any attempted to get in?"

"That they have, but their efforts were foiled before they got a word of the language!" replied the Prince, a note of triumph in his voice.

"How? Tell me. How came it?" Satan was all attention now.

"Why," began the Prince, "I was roaming back and forth within my domains, having penetrated far into the Arctic Circle in order to visit one of the most isolated tribes, when suddenly I was amazed to hear that two missionaries were on their way from across the water, that they had landed, and with their dog sleighs were already well into the heart of my kingdom, Alaska, making for a large tribe of Eskimo just within the Arctic Circle."

"Yes, and what didst thou do?" broke in Satan, impatient to hear the climax.

"First of all, I gathered together the hosts of darkness under my command and held a council. Many suggestions were made. Finally it was agreed that the easiest way was to freeze them to death.

"Finding that they were that day leaving for the distant tribe and that it would in all probability take them a full month to cross the frozen ice fields that intervened, we at once began operations.

"With hearts burdened to make the message known, they started. Manfully they 'mushed' along. But when about a week out, suddenly one day their food sleigh ran over thin ice, which broke beneath its weight, and was almost immediately lost.

"Weary and tired, they bravely plodded on only to realize that they were in a helpless condition, and still over three weeks from their destination. They were new to the great Northland, and were no match for it.

"Finally, when they were out of food, tired and weary in body, and almost ready to give up, I gave the word of command, and in a short time the wind began to blow a hurricane, the snow came down in a blinding blizzard, and before morning, thanks to the fact that thou, O my lord, art the Prince of the Powers of the Air, they were cold and stiff in death."

"Excellent! Splendid! Thou didst serve me well," commented the fallen cherub, with a gratified expression on his once beautiful countenance.

"And what hast thou to report?" he continued, turning to the Prince of Tibet, who had listened with evident satisfaction to the conversation.

"I, too, have a story that will fill Your Majesty with delight," responded the one addressed.

"Ha! Has an attempt been made to invade thy kingdom as well, my Prince?" inquired Satan with growing interest.

"That there has," responded the Prince.

"How? Tell me about it," commanded Satan, instantly on the alert.

"I was attending to my duties in the heart of Tibet," explained the Prince, "when news reached me of a Society organized specially to get the Gospel to my kingdom. Thou mayest well know, my lord, that I was at once on the alert.

I called my forces together to discuss the whole situation, and we presently agreed on a plan that promised success.

"With great determination, two men sent out by the Society travelled across China and boldly passing over the border, entered the Forbidden Land. We allowed them to advance about three days' journey, and then, just as it was growing dark, two savage dogs, such as are found all over the country, sprang upon them. Most desperately they fought for their lives, but finally one was dragged down and killed. The other, protected by invisible forces which we were unable to overcome, somehow escaped."

"Escaped!" cried Satan, making a hideous gesture. "Escaped! Did he get the message to them?"

"No, my lord," responded the Prince of Tibet, in a tone of assurance. "He had no chance. Before he could learn a word of the language, our hosts had him set upon by the natives themselves. He was quickly tried and sentenced. Oh, it was a scene that would have filled Your Majesty with delight. They sewed him up in a wet yak skin and put him out in the sun to bake. For three days he remained there, his bones slowly cracking as the skin shrank, until finally life ceased."

The room had been filling fast while the Prince of Tibet was speaking, and at the conclusion of his report a great cheer rose from the entire assembly, while all bowed to the majestic figure of Satan, still beautiful, in spite of the ravages of sin.

But a moment later, the cheering subsided, hushed by a wave of Satan's hand.

"And what hast thou to report?" he asked, turning to another fallen angel. "Art thou still master of Afghanistan, my Prince?"

"That I am, Your Majesty," replied the one addressed, "though were it not for my faithful followers, I doubt if it would be so."

"Ah! Has an attempt been made on thy domains also?" exclaimed Satan in a loud voice.

"Yes, my lord," responded the Prince. "But listen and I will tell all."

With a wave of his hand for silence, he began:

"We watched their advance; there were four of them—all zealous to make Him known.

"Thou knowest, my lord, of the sign that meets the traveller just inside the border of my kingdom. It reads as follows:

"*It is absolutely forbidden to cross this border into Afghanistan territory.*

"Well, they knelt down around it and prayed, but, in spite of this, our valiant forces prevailed. Fifty feet from the sign, on a pile or rocks, sits an Afghan guard, rifle in hand. After praying, the little company stepped boldly over the border and entered the Forbidden Land. The guard allowed them to advance twenty paces, then, like a flash of lightning, three shots were fired and three of the company lay on the ground, two of them dead, the third wounded. His comrade hastily dragged the wounded man back to the border, where, after a short sickness, he died, while he himself lost heart and fled from the country."

Prolonged cheering followed this recital, and great joy filled every heart, Satan's most of all, for was he not still in possession of the Closed Lands, and had he not triumphed on every field? The message, thanks to his countless hordes, had still been kept out, nor had the dreaded Name yet been heard.

"Wilt thou not tell us, oh, thou Mighty One, why thou art so anxious to keep the knowledge from these our empires? Knowest thou not that the kingdoms of the Prince of India, the Prince of China and His Royal Highness the Prince of Africa, are being invaded by strong forces, and that men are turning to Christ every day?"

"Ah, yes, full well I know. But listen all, and I will explain why I am so jealous for the Closed Lands," answered Satan, while all bent forward to hear.

"There are several prophecies, perhaps best summed up in this one," he began, "which reads as follows: 'This Gospel of the kingdom shall be preached in all the world for a witness unto all nations; and then shall the end come.' Now it is very clear," he continued in a low tone, "that God is visiting the Gentiles, 'to take out of them a people for His name,' and 'after this,' He says, 'I will return'; and the Great Commission implies that disciples are to be made from among all nations.

"Now," he exclaimed with indignation, "Jesus Christ cannot return to reign until every nation has heard the Good News, for it reads, 'I beheld a great multitude, which no man could number, of all nations, and kindreds, and people, and tongues' (Rev. 7:9). Hence, it matters not how many missionaries are sent to countries already evangelized, nor how many converts are made, for not until the message of the Gospel has been proclaimed in Alaska, Tibet, Afghanistan and our other domains, where it has never yet been heard, will He return to reign."

"Then," broke in the Prince of Nepal, "if we can keep every messenger out of the Closed Lands, we can prevent His coming to reign on the earth and so frustrate the purposes of the Most High."

"And that we will," cried the proud Prince of Cambodia. "Only the other day," he continued, "a missionary himself wrote saying, 'At this time we do not know of a single Cambodian who has a saving knowledge of our Saviour Jesus Christ.' We will see to it, Your Majesty, that not one escapes."

"That is good," said Satan. "Let us be even more vigilant and frustrate every attempt to enter the Closed Lands."

As the great plan dawned upon them, they shouted with glee, and hurried back to their empires, more determined than ever to prevent the escape of a single soul.

Fifty years passed. Restlessly His Satanic Majesty paced back and forth. Dark, foreboding frowns passed over his countenance. It was quite apparent that something of an unusual nature was troubling him.

"It must not be," he muttered to himself. "And the very plan, too," he continued in a louder tone. "Yes, the very plan. They seem to have caught a vision of it at last. 'Evangelize,' 'pioneer,' I don't like these words. And then that written statement of theirs, 'The objects sought by the Society include the following: To hasten the return of our Lord by following His programme for this age which is to "preach the Gospel in all the world for a witness to all nations," and, "to take out of them a people for His name," as He said, "Go ye into all the world, and preach the Gospel to every creature." Its aim is to engage in only such activities as contribute to world evangelism. Its missionary policy is to avoid duplicating existing Gospel agencies abroad by directing its efforts to pioneer service among peoples, tribes and nations where Christ is not named.'

" 'Regions beyond,' 'unoccupied areas,' 'pioneer service among peoples, tribes and nations where Christ is not named!' And 'to hasten the return of our Lord by following His programme for this age.' Then that phrase of theirs, 'Bringing back the King.' 'The King!' 'The King!' It shall not be. I must frustrate their purposes! 'The King!' What will happen to me when He comes? I must call a council immediately."

In a few minutes they were all present. From the uttermost parts they came—mighty fallen angels, dignitaries, princes, captains, world rulers of the darkness of this age—in countless multitudes they gathered around their lord, who stood with pent-up rage in their midst. Silence, silence like the silence of death, reigned. Presently Satan spoke:

"Prince of Alaska, stand thou forth!"

Trembling and afraid, with a shrinking form unlike his appearance of fifty years before, he approached his dread monarch.

"Prince of Alaska," inquired Satan, "have they entered yet?"

"Yes, my lord, they have," slowly responded the Prince, with a look of fear, hardly raising his eyes.

"How! What!" thundered Satan, scarcely able to control himself. "Why didst thou not better guard my empire?"

"We did our best, Your Majesty, but it was all of no avail. Word somehow got back; the frozen bodies of the first two were discovered. It set the whole Church on fire. Others ventured. Several we destroyed. More grew discouraged and turned back. But finally, in spite of all we could do, they got through. Guarded and protected by legions of angels, they entered and stayed; nor could we drive them out. And today, there are hundreds of Eskimos in the kingdom of God, while thousands have heard the Tidings!"

The scene that followed beggars all description. Satan fumed and fairly bellowed out his rage. The very air seemed alive with a million spirits. His leading princes cowed before him and sought to get away from his terrible eyes.

"Prince of Tibet, stand thou forth!" roared the enraged fiend, a moment later.

"Thou hast a better report to give, I hope," he continued, as that renowned leader stepped forward.

"No, my lord, I have fared but little better," answered the Prince.

"What!" stormed Satan. "Have any heard the Name in thy domain, O Prince?"

"No power at my disposal could prevent it," responded the Prince quietly. "We did our best. All our forces toiled day and night to overcome them. It seems there is a movement raised up for the sole purpose of going where no one else has gone and preaching in so-called unoccupied areas of the world, whose leader, the Prince of China, with his forces, tried to destroy, but in vain. Protected by legions of angels, he lived. Dogs were turned on them. We filled the priests with deadly hatred towards them. Pitfalls were laid for them on every side. Starvation methods were adopted. Disease did its part. But it was useless. On and on they pressed, until, today, there are scores of Tibetans lost to us forever, and thousands of others have heard the News. Far and wide, witness has been borne."

At that, Satan's rage knew no bounds. Without a moment's delay, he turned and gave his final command:

"Prince of Afghanistan, stand thou forth!"

There was a moment's hesitation; then, with slow steps and downcast eyes, the one addressed responded, and stood trembling before his sovereign.

"Prince of Afghanistan," began Satan again, "thou hast guarded well my domains. Shouldst thou also fail me, I know not where to turn."

There was no reply. Silence held the great audience spellbound.

"Speak, O Prince. Have they entered?"

"They have, my lord."

"Prince of Afghanistan," exclaimed the fiend, springing forward with fury in every expression, "hast thou not been true?"

"Yes, my lord, I have, but it was no use. We did our best. Up until a year ago, not a soul heard. Then two young men were sent by that Pioneer Society, and——"

"Curse them!" broke in Satan.

"The whole Church prayed," continued the Prince. "They all seem to know that He will not come to reign until the Gospel has been preached in every tongue. Angels guarded. Oh, yes, we fought, but could not withstand them. On they came, and a week ago one man accepted the Christ and several others have already heard."

"And now," roared Satan, "all is lost! Thousands have been saved in India and China, but the news I have just heard is the worst of all. He may come now. At least it will not be long, for with the vision of these people, every tribe, tongue and nation will be reached. And then, woe, woe is me!"

CHAPTER II

WHAT IS THE SUPREME TASK OF THE CHURCH?

TURN WITH me, if you will, to Ezekiel 3, verses 17 to 19. I am going to change some of the words in this passage in order to bring it up to date. Note carefully the changes. I want to make it applicable to the mission field. Now let us read, beginning at verse 17:

"Christian worker, I have made thee a watchman: therefore hear the word at my mouth, and give warning from me. When I say unto the heathen, Thou shalt surely die; and thou givest him not warning, nor speakest to warn the heathen from his heathenish way, to save his life, the same heathen shall die in his iniquity; *BUT his blood will I require at thine hand.* Yet if thou warn the heathen, and he turn not from his heathenism, nor from his heathenish way, he shall die in his iniquity; but thou hast delivered thy soul." His blood will I require at thine hand.

Down through the years my life has been tremendously motivated by great missionary mottoes. May I give you one now that perhaps has meant more to me than any other. It is this, "The supreme task of the Church is the evangelization of the world." I believe that with all my heart. The most important work of the Church of Jesus Christ is world evangelization.

WORLD

I am going to take three words in this motto and emphasize them one by one. First of all, let me take the last word, the word "world." "The supreme task of the Church is the evangelization of the *world.*" When God loved, He loved a world. When He gave His Son, He gave His Son for a world.

17

When Jesus Christ died, He died for a world. God's vision is a world vision. That is the vision He wants us to have.

So many of us are localized in our outlook. We see only our own community, our own village or town, and we never see beyond. There are those who think only of their own church and have no interest in what others are doing. Then there are some who have a larger vision. They see an entire city or province and they are ready to give their money and to work for its evangelization. But they, too, are local in their outlook, for they never see beyond the boundaries of the city or province in which they live. Then there are those who have a still larger vision. They see an entire country and they are ready to work for its evangelization. But even they are local in their outlook, for they never see beyond the boundaries of the country in which they live. There are those, however, who have a still larger vision. They see a continent and they are ready to do all they can for the evangelization of their continent. Yet even they are local in their outlook for they never see beyond the boundaries of their continent. Then there are those who see an entire world. They see Europe, Asia, Africa, North and South America and the islands of the seas. They have God's vision and that is the vision He wants us to have, a world vision.

Why is it that so many of us are local in our outlook? Why do we think only of ourselves? Is God more interested in these black people living here than He is in those yellow people living there? Is He more concerned about those brown people than He is about those who are white? Is it because we are so near-sighted that we do not have a world vision? When I was leaving Jamaica I stepped into a plane. First of all I saw only the local surroundings. Then as I rose higher, I saw fields and farm houses. As I got higher still I was able to see valleys and mountains in the distance. Finally I could look down upon the entire island of Jamaica, lying like a jewel in the bosom of the Caribbean; and if I could have gone high enough, I could have seen all the islands of the West Indies at a single glance.

God, from His vantage point, can look down upon an entire world and see every country, continent and island at the same time. If we could only get far enough away, we could see the world as Jesus saw it. But some of us have never travelled and we have never listened to those who have travelled. We do not study geography. We know but little of what lies beyond.

Why is it that we think we are the people and that we are more important than any of the other peoples of the world? Everywhere I go I hear that sentiment expressed. When I was in Great Britain I found the people there saying, "We're the people." When I was in Australia and South Africa, it was the same, "We're the people." As I travel through the United States I hear it on every side, "We're the people." I was once on a little bit of an island in the Pacific and even there the natives were saying, "We're the people." They used to talk to me something like this, "You Americans," they would say, "why is it that you live away out on the outer fringe of civilization? Why don't you live nearer to the centre of things?" The idea was that we Britishers and Americans live afar off, out on the outer fringe of civilization, while they, those natives on that island in the Pacific, live at the hub. The trouble was they were localized in their outlook, they did not have a world vision. They thought they were the most important people of the world.

Is it, I wonder, because we think we are the most numerous? Some of us, I am afraid, do not realize that there are other nations in the world with even larger populations, that we are not the only pebbles on the beach.

I was in the Dutch East Indies and I travelled through the island of Java. I found that I could cross it, from one end to the other, in about twelve hours and from North to South in about four hours. Will you believe me when I tell you that Java is one of the most densely populated spots on the face of the earth? There are 75 million people on that little island. I could put sixty Javas in Canada and have lots of room to spare, yet Java contains nearly one-third of the population of the United States. If God is interested in numbers, then God is more interested in Java than He is in my country, the Dominion of Canada, for whereas there are twenty-three million people in Canada, there are, as I have already stated, 75 million in Java.

If God is interested in numbers, then He is more interested in the United States than He is in Java, for whereas there are 75 million in Java, there are two hundred and sixteen million in the United States of America. But again, if God is interested in numbers, then He is more interested in Russia than He is in the United States, for whereas there are two hundred and sixteen million in the States, there are 250 million in Russia. Russia is the largest white nation on the face of the earth— 250 million. But once again, if God is interested in numbers, then He is more interested in India than He is in Russia, for whereas there are 250 million in Russia, there are six hundred million in India, over twice the population. But, last of all, if God is interested in numbers, then He is more interested in China than He is in India, for whereas there are six hundred million in India, there are more than eight hundred million in China, the largest nation in the world. Every fourth baby born into the world is born a Chinese. Someone has said, "God must love the Chinese because He has made so many of them."

And my country, the Dominion of Canada, viewed from the standpoint of numbers, is only a little pin point on the map. And if the waters of the Atlantic and the waters of the Pacific should rise overnight and submerge Canada, I suppose next morning there would be a report in the American newspapers about an inch deep, stating, "Last night Canada disappeared from the family of nations." That is all we amount to. We just don't amount to anything when it comes to numbers. Why then should we conceive of ourselves as *the* people? Why should we be local in our outlook? Why should we think of ourselves as more important than any of the other peoples of the world? Why should God be more interested in us than in other nations? Oh that He would give us a world vision, that we might work for the evangelization of the entire world, the world for which Christ died, and that we might see the world as He sees it.

SUPREME

Now let us look at another word in our motto, the word "supreme." "The *supreme* task of the Church is the evangelization of the world."

If world evangelization is our most important work, then when a missionary convention is held we should lay everything else aside and be present at every session, otherwise we are putting something else first, and we do not believe that it is more important than anything else. We show by our actions that we put missions second.

In the second place, if world evangelization comes first, then we should concentrate on giving to missions and let others who do not have the vision, contribute to other things. There will always be plenty for the home work, for there are always those who put the home work first. The many worthwhile objects here at home will be cared for, since only the minority will be interested in the supreme task of the Church.

If we put missions first, then we will give more to missions than to anything else. Otherwise something else takes first place. There are business men here and each one has his own business enterprise. Now there is one department in your business that you look upon as more important than any other department. Where then do you put most of your surplus money? Why, into that most important department, of course. Why do you do that? Because you want to develop the most important department of your business enterprise. So it is with missions. If world evangelism is the most important work of the Church, then we should put most of our money into this most important department. Otherwise, we do not put missions first and we do not believe that world evangelization is the supreme task of the Church. I find very few ministers who really believe that the evangelization of the world is their most important work.

This leads me to say that every church should spend more on missions than it spends on itself. That is only logical. If we believe that world evangelization comes first, then we should invest more money in the regions beyond than we use for ourselves here at home.

"But," you ask, "what about your church? What about The Peoples Church in Toronto of which you are pastor? Does your church send more to the foreign field than it spends on itself?" I am glad to be able to say that there never has been a year since I have been Pastor of The Peoples Church when we have used anything like as much on ourselves at home as we have sent to the foreign fields of earth.

Years ago I asked our auditors, through our treasurer, two questions. First, "How much did we spend on ourselves last year?" After they had examined the books I got the answer. "Dr. Smith," they said, "last year, you used $53,000 on your work at home." Then I asked my second question, "How much did we send to the foreign field? How much was raised for missions?" Again I got the answer. "Last year, you gave $318,000 to missions." "Fine," I said, "that is the way it always has been and that is the way it should be." And if the time ever comes when the officials of The Peoples Church decide to spend more here at home and less on missions, they will get my resignation without a moment's hesitation. I would not want to be the pastor of a church that would use more here at home than it sent to the regions beyond.

When I moved The Peoples Church to Gerrard Street, many years ago now, I was told everything except one thing, and on the Sunday morning that I was to preach my first sermon, the treasurer approached me with a very grim expression on his countenance. "Dr. Smith," he said, "we have told you everything there is to tell you about this church except one thing." Then he paused. I waited for him to continue with what he was going to say. In a moment he went on. "This church," he said, "is in debt. We have some unpaid bills and we have nothing in the treasury." And then he looked at me as though he expected me to put my hand in my pocket, take out the money and give it to him, telling him to run away and pay the bills.

Instead, I turned and went into the pulpit and as I went I prayed. "Lord," I said, "I have been wanting to find out for a long time whether or not a certain passage in Thy Word is true." True, I meant, from a practical standpoint. I referred to that verse, "Seek ye first the kingdom of God (the extension of God's kingdom world-wide) and all these things shall be added unto you." That morning I preached a missionary sermon.

Sunday evening came. It was my first Sunday. I should have brought an evangelistic message, but again I felt led to speak on missions, and I did so. Then I asked the people to come back every night that week. They came, and on Monday night I gave them missions again. On Tuesday they got another dose of missions. Wednesday night they had to listen to still another missionary address. On Thursday night it was missions again. By Friday they were coming in increasing numbers, perhaps more out of curiosity than for any other reason, and once again they got a dose of missions.

Then, I suppose they folded their arms, saying one to another, "This new pastor of ours, we cannot understand him. He doesn't seem to have any sermons except on missions. But the second Sunday is coming. Perhaps then he will really start to preach."

The second Sunday came. I can remember it as though it were yesterday. At the morning service I made an announcement. "We are going to hold three services today," I said, "and take up three missionary offerings: one this morning, another this afternoon and the last one tonight." Some of them seemed to look at me in amazement, but I had started my work, assisted by one missionary, with an attempt at a missionary convention, and I was determined to see it through. That morning I spoke on missions and took up a missionary offering. I did the same in the afternoon and again at night. Here I was, hardly saying a word about home needs and yet taking all the money I could get from them for missions. But now for the sequel.

They became so interested, so aroused, so awakened, that they came in ever-increasing numbers. Souls were saved and in a very short time every seat was taken. Before long they had caught the vision and they began to give, to give as they had never given before, and in a few weeks, without having to say hardly anything about the local obligations, every debt was paid, every bill met, and from that day to this we have not known the meaning of the word "debt" in connection with our work. We discovered that when we put first things first, God works.

The trouble with the average church is that the cart is put before the horse and then the pastor is told to get up on the seat and drive, and of course he finds the going hard. If only we would reverse the order and accept God's plan, we would get somewhere and the going would be easy. Seek first the extension of God's kingdom world-wide, and all things will be added. God's programme never fails.

CHURCH

The third word I want to emphasize is the word "Church." "The supreme task of the *Church* is the evangelization of the world." When I think of the church I think of the whole church, and not merely of a department or an organization in the church. For instance, we do not have any Women's Missionary Society in The Peoples Church. We never have had such an organization and we never will. Not because I am against such a society. I thank God for every Women's Missionary Society. Sometimes the only missionary light that shines is the light that shines from a Women's Missionary Society. But I can show you in two minutes why it would be impossible for us to have such an organization.

Suppose I were to gather together a little group of women, a dozen or more, and suppose I were to say to those women, "Now you are to become a Women's Missionary Society, and your work will be the work of evangelizing the world. That is all you have to do, just evangelize the world." What then would I be saying to everyone else and to all the other organizations in the church? I would be saying, "This is not the most important work of the church. It is only a side issue, just one of the many departments of church work. Let these women look after it. They can take care of the evangelization of the world; and the rest of us—those of us who are men— we will do something really worthy of our manhood."

No, my friends! Every man in my church is a member of the Women's Missionary Society. And I see to it, as far as possible, that every one of the 120 members of my choir accepts his or her responsibility; that each one of my elders, managers and deacons, more than two hundred, shoulders the burden; that every usher, every Sunday School teacher and officer and every boy and girl, contributes to missions. We do not have the parents give for the children. We teach the children to give for themselves. From the time they are seven years of age, they are taught to give systematically. Then when they grow up we have no trouble with them. They have learned how to give.

Last year our Sunday School gave $211,000 to missions. Our elders gave $90,000 and our choir $36,000.

This work is far too important to hand over to any one organization. It belongs to the whole church, and when every-one catches the vision and everyone does something, then our goal is reached and our budget met. Our motto is, "Every Christian a missionary." It is the work of the whole church.

How is it Done?

Everywhere I go I am asked the question, "How do you get such offerings? Where does the money come from? You must have a church of millionaires." That is what the editor of Canada's Roman Catholic paper thought when he saw the report in the daily press. He wrote and asked me if it were so, and when I replied in the negative, he was astonished. He wrote a long article in his Roman Catholic publication, stating that one Protestant church, led, as he said, by a zealous pastor, gave more to missions than all the Catholic churches from Ontario to the Coast put together. "We," he said, "are the true custodians of the Faith, and yet we allow one Protestant church to outdo us. Shame on us." His thought, of course, was to stir up the Catholics to do more. No, we have no millionaires. As a matter of fact, we do not have any real wealth in our church. Our gifts come from a multitude of ordinary people.

At one time an official of the Foreign Mission Board of a large denomination asked me for the secret, and wanted to know why the giving of his denomination had decreased. "Dr. So-and-So," I said, "you have put missions in the budget and you appeal to the people for a dead, cold budget and then you divide the money as you see fit. It will never do. World-wide evangelism is too important to be put in a budget. You will have to pull it out of the budget and put it on the plat-form where the people can see it. You will have to go back to the great missionary rallies of the days of the Student Volunteer Movement, when multitudes of young men and women were inspired to go. People will never give to a budget. They must have inspiration." He admitted that I was right.

How do we get it? Perhaps if I were to tell you how we do NOT get it, it would help. We do not raise it by means of suppers, bazaars, concerts, rummage sales, or oyster stews. Not because I am against these methods, but because they will not work. What does a business man do when he runs across a method that will not work? He scraps it, does he not? Now listen. I am responsible, humanly speaking, for the per-sonal support of three hundred and fifty missionaries. Every month of my life I have to get more than $25,000, or humanly speaking, they will starve. How many of you busi-ness men carry as heavy a responsibility? What would you do if you had to get $25,000 every month, and if three hun-dred and fifty workers were dependent upon it? May I pause long enough to say that never once has God failed. Whether I am at home or on some foreign field, or holding evangelistic campaigns in Great Britain or Australia, the money comes in and the allowances go out.

Now tell me if you ever knew a rummage sale to produce $25,000. If not, then what good is it? Do you blame me for scrapping a method that will not produce what I need? I have never known it to happen. Well then, what do I do? I turn to another method, of course, a method that will bring in the amount needed. A lot of people have an idea that when George Mueller died, George Mueller's God died. God is not dead. Elijah's God still lives today. He can work the necessary miracle. "Said I not unto thee, that, if thou would believe, thou shouldest see the glory of God? All things are possible to him that believeth."

Every year for 50 years, we have held a missionary convention. It used to last for one week. Then, for several years, four weeks and five Sundays. After giving the people a vision of missions, morning, afternoon and night, we take up a faith-promise offering. Our people indicate the amount they will contribute during the next twelve months. Does it work? Let me give you two examples.

Park Street Church, Boston, asked me to hold an evangelistic campaign. I did so. The auditorium was crowded, with many standing on the steps, and score upon scores, mostly young people, found Christ. Dr. Harold Ockenga, the Pastor, asked me to come into his office. "Dr. Smith," he said, "this church has never had a missionary convention in the one hundred and thirty-five years of its history. We understand that you hold one every year. Would you be willing to come to Park Street and hold one for us?" I asked Dr. Ockenga how much his church was, at that time, contributing to missions. His answer was, $3,200 a year. Next year I took a group of missionaries and held a convention in Park Street Church. I went back every year for six years. Last year Park Street gave over $300,000 to missions.

The other example is my own church. When I held my first convention the offering was $3,500. In 1972 it was $597,000. My son, Dr. Paul B. Smith, the present pastor, took it up.

The total offerings have now run well over 8 million dollars. That is what conventions and Faith-Promise Offerings do. Today, it is over $700,000 a year.

There is a legend told concerning the return of Jesus to Heaven. Meeting Gabriel, He stated that He had completed His divinely appointed task.

"And what is your plan?" inquired Gabriel. "How is the Gospel to be spread? Did you leave a strong organization on the earth with well defined plans?"

"No," answered the Saviour. "I left no organization, only a small company of disciples, mostly of very humble birth. They are to tell the world."

"But suppose they fail you," persisted Gabriel, "what plan have you then?"

"I have no other," replied the Saviour, sorrowfully.

Some day millions upon millions from heathenism will march by the throne and, pointing a finger of scorn at us, they will cry: "No man cared for my soul." And then you and I will try to justify ourselves by exclaiming, "But, Lord, am I my brother's keeper?" And God will answer, "The voice of thy brother's blood crieth unto me from Africa, from China, from the islands of the sea." *The voice of thy brother's blood.* Yes, and you will go into Heaven, saved, but—with blood on your hands, the blood of those you might have won had you gone or sent someone in your place.

It is no light thing to be a watchman. "His blood will I require at thine hand." The Supreme Task of the Church is the Evangelization of the World. What are you going to do about it?

CHAPTER III

HOW GOD CALLED ME TO A WORLD-WIDE MINISTRY

LET US turn to the Gospel according to Matthew, chapter nine, verses thirty-five to thirty-eight: "And Jesus went about all the cities and villages . . ." Note, if you will, that He went about *all* the cities and villages. He did not settle down in any one community. Jesus never became a pastor. He was continually on the go. "Jesus went about all the cities and villages, preaching the gospel.

"But—when He saw the multitudes, He was moved with compassion." What is compassion? Compassion is not pity. Compassion is love in action. Are we moved with compassion? If we are we will do something about it.

"Then saith He unto His disciples, the harvest truly is plenteous, but the labourers are few." This, then, is the problem. And the problem of His day is the problem of our day— a plenteous harvest, few labourers. Now for the solution to the problem: "Pray ye therefore the Lord of the harvest, that He will send forth labourers into His harvest."

COULD I STAY IN CANADA?

Years ago I went through the Bible to see if I could stay in Canada and still obey God. Would it be possible, I asked myself, for me to enjoy a comfortable pastorate; never cross the boundaries of my country and still carry out my Lord's commands? Would God be satisfied?

And as I studied the Bible I found such expressions as these: "All nations; all the world; every creature; every kindred, and tongue, and people, and nation; the uttermost part of the earth." In other words, the Gospel, I discovered,

29

was to be given to the entire world. Every nation, kindred, tongue, and people, must hear it.

When I saw that, this then was the question I asked: Do all nations live in Canada? If they do, and if there are no nations living beyond the boundaries of the Dominion, then I can stay in my own country, preach the Gospel here and never once cross the borders; but,—if *one* nation lives beyond the boundaries of Canada, then I am in duty bound to leave my country, cross the boundaries and go to that nation. And if I cannot, then I must send out substitutes. And if I do neither, I will be a missing Christian in the day of rewards.

My friend, what about you? You know that the Gospel must be given to all nations, to all the world, to every kindred and tongue and people, to the uttermost part of the earth. What are you doing about it? What are you going to do? Either you must go yourself or else you must send someone in your place, and woe betide you if you do nothing. God's orders must be obeyed, His commands carried out, and there is no way to evade the issue.

I Tried to Go

When I was eighteen years of age I went to the Indians of British Columbia. I lived in a little shack on an Indian Reserve all alone, up near Alaska, between three and four thousand miles from home. I stayed away for over a year; then, realizing that I needed more education, I returned at last to civilization and settled down to a five-year course of theology, finally graduating and being ordained to the Gospel ministry, after which I took a year of post-graduate work.

I then applied to the Presbyterian Board of Foreign Missions for work in India. My case was considered very carefully. I appeared personally before the Board and at last a decision was reached. I was rejected. The Board felt that I would not be suitable for missionary work, and so I was turned down.

I turned to work at home—became pastor of Dale Presbyterian Church, Toronto, and later of the Alliance Tabernacle;

but I was not satisfied. I knew that I had to do something. I had seen the vision. Finally, I struck out on my own, going to the Russian mission fields of Europe and preaching to vast multitudes all over Latvia, Esthonia, and Poland, winning many souls for Christ. Finally, one day, after having preached till I was worn out, I fainted dead away and returned home.

All over the United States and Canada I travelled, holding evangelistic campaigns. Finally I felt the urge again and this time went to Spain, but again I became ill and had to come back.

Then I founded The Peoples Church in Toronto. That was in the year 1928. Four years after, the urge came upon me once more and I left for Africa. By horseback I penetrated back into the interior, in the company of Dr. Thomas Lambie, riding some thirty miles a day, finally collapsing in the long grass of Africa; and after a very serious illness that lasted for six weeks, I was brought back once again to civilization.

By this time I was beginning to feel that the Board had been right after all and that I was not fitted for missionary work. However, I had seen the vision, I knew that other nations had to hear the Gospel, and in 1938 I went once again, determined to do my part, if at all possible, to help evangelize the world. This time I left for the far Pacific, and after travelling by steamer for thirty-one days, day and night, I found myself preaching to the cannibals, the savages and the Christians of the Solomon Islands. At length, however, I contracted malaria fever, which lasted for three years, and again and again, month after month, laid me low. Finally, one day, Dr. Northcote Deck and the other missionaries put me on a steamer and sent me back to my work in Toronto.

But I did not stop until I had visited 70 different countries and I am still going.

I TURNED TO SUBSTITUTES

In the early days of my ministry, realizing that I could not go myself, I turned to substitutes. One day I approached

Rev. J. H. W. Cook, the leader of the Evangelical Union of South America.

"You want to send out some new missionaries?" I said.

"Yes," he replied. "We have five ready to go."

"Why don't you send them?" I inquired.

"We do not have the money," was his reply.

"If I can succeed in raising the funds for their transportation, will you allow me to support them?" I asked him.

His face lit up as he responded in the affirmative.

Never will I forget the day I placed those five missionaries on the platform of The Peoples Church and challenged the congregation to send them out. They did so. Then the five became ten; the ten, twenty; the twenty, forty; the forty, one hundred; the one hundred, two hundred; the two hundred, three hundred and fifty. Now we have an army of labourers serving as our substitutes on some forty different foreign fields, under thirty-five Faith Missionary Societies, and we contribute toward their "personal" support.

But . . . I am not satisfied. I am praying constantly and this is my prayer: "Lord, let me live, if it be Thy will, until we have four hundred missionaries on the foreign fields of earth." I feel that that is the number that The Peoples Church should help support and I will never be satisfied until we have at least that many missionaries in the regions beyond.

This is what I am living for. I am a pastor and an evangelist second; I am a missionary first. I am a hymn-writer second; a missionary first. I am an author second; I am a missionary first. I tried to go myself; as a matter of fact, I went, but each time it seemed that I had to come back. I knew then that there was only one thing left to do; namely, to send others. That is why I travel all over the United States of America, the Dominion of Canada, Australia, New Zealand, South Africa and Great Britain. I go in order to hold missionary conventions and to challenge young people. I must do all I can to find and send substitutes.

THE NEXT TOWNS

A little while ago, I read in your hearing the story of how Jesus went to all the cities and villages. Do you remember the time He disappeared, after having ministered in a certain town; and do you recall how the disciples went in search of Him, in the early hours of the morning, and how at last they found Him on the top of a mountain engaged in prayer?

"Master," they cried, "the people are waiting for you. There are many more sick to be healed. Come back and finish your work. There are still others in the town in which you ministered yesterday, who want to hear you."

Yes, and I can imagine the Master replying, as with a far-away look in His eyes He gazed out over the valleys and the mountains in the distance, in these words: "I must preach in the *next* towns for therefore am I sent." He was thinking, as He always did, of the next towns, and the next, and the next. He was thinking of those towns in which He had never yet ministered; and He wanted to get to them that they, too, might hear the Gospel. He was ever mindful of "the other sheep."

Paul had the same vision. He talked about "the regions beyond," the unoccupied areas. He said he wanted to go to Spain and to Rome. He, too, realized that the Gospel had to be taken to "all the world."

Do you know that the whole of North Africa was at one time evangelized and that hundreds of Christian churches dotted the landscape? Do you realize that some of our greatest theologians came from North Africa in the early centuries of the Christian era? But what happened? North Africa became Mohammedan and for hundreds of years there was hardly a trace of Christianity left. The candles burned lower and lower until at last they burned out and the light that had shone so brightly was extinguished. How explain it? Let me tell you.

The religious leaders and theologians in North Africa got into controversy one with another and instead of preaching the

Gospel and evangelizing, they started theological discussions and argued with each other over Christian doctrine. What should they have done? They should have gone to the next towns south and then the next towns south of those. And what would have happened? Within a very short time they would have reached Capetown, and the whole of Africa would have been evangelized hundreds of years ago. Africa might have been sending missionaries to Europe and even to America.

That, my brethren, may happen here. Yea, it is happening here. There are churches today in the United States and Canada as well as in Great Britain, Australia, and New Zealand—hundreds of them—that have become mere social clubs, and if the Church of Jesus Christ does not awaken and give the Gospel to the whole world, what happened to Africa will happen here. "The light that shines farthest, shines brightest nearest home."

"The Field is the World"

"But," you ask, "why go before all have been saved here? There is so much to be done at home. Why not complete the work in the homeland before going to the foreign field?" Everywhere I go that question is asked. Let me answer it by asking three or four others:

First.—Why did David Livingstone leave Scotland and go to Africa before everyone in Scotland had become a Christian? Why? There are still thousands in Scotland who have not even yet decided for Christ. And yet, years ago, Livingstone left his own land and went to dark, benighted Africa. I ask you—why?

Second.—Why did William Carey leave England and go to India before everyone in England had been Christianized? Why? There are still some in England who have not been won to Christ.

Third.—Why did Judson leave America and go to Burma before everyone in America had been brought to Christ? Why? There are still a few in the States who have not been Christianized.

LASTLY.—Why did the Apostle Paul leave for Europe before Palestine had *heard* the Gospel? Why? Paul, you remember, deliberately turned from his own country and went to our forefathers in Europe in order to evangelize them. Why, I ask, did he do it? Ought he not to have stayed in Palestine, at least until they had heard the message?

My friends, there is only one answer and I give it in the words of the Bible: "The field is the world." The United States of America is not the world. Great Britain is not the world. The field is the whole world. You never in your life heard of a farmer working in one little corner of his field. The farmer works the whole field. The United States is but one corner; Canada is but a little corner. The world, the whole world, must be evangelized. And since "the field is the world," we have no choice but to go to every part of it. The work is one and it must be done, not corner by corner, but as a whole.

The tobacco firms have their agents in the most distant places. Millions of cigarettes are given away to create new appetites. Do you mean to say that the reason for it is because there is no longer any demand at home? Of course not. The demand here—especially since women have stepped down from the high pedestal upon which they once stood and have taken to cigarette smoking—is greater than ever. Yet the tobacco firms are already sending their missionaries into foreign lands. They want new markets. They are wiser than we are, for that, after all, is God's plan and we would do well to emulate them. It has never been God's will that we should remain at home until the work here is finished. He wants us to go to the entire world, to work the whole field simultaneously.

Do you know what you are saying when you say you do not believe in missions? You are saying that Paul made a mistake; that he should have left your forefathers in Europe, pagans; that it would have been better if he had stayed at home in Palestine so that you might have remained in heathenism. Is that what you think? Are you sorry you are not still a heathen? You must be if you do not believe in missions.

Do you remember when the Lord Jesus Christ fed the five thousand? Do you recall how He had them sit down, row upon row, on the green grass? Then do you remember how He took the loaves and fishes and blessed them and then broke them and gave them to His disciples? And do you remember how the disciples started at one end of the front row and went right along that front row giving everyone a helping? Then do you recall how they turned right around and started back along that front row again, asking everyone to take a second helping? Do you remember?

No!—a thousand times—no! Had they done that, those in the back rows would have been rising up and protesting most vigorously. "Here," they would have been saying, "come back here. Give us a helping. We have not had any yet. We are starving; it isn't right; it isn't fair. Why should those people in the front rows have a second helping before we have had a first?"

And they would have been right. We talk about the second blessing. They haven't had the first blessing yet. We talk about the second coming of Christ. They haven't heard about the first coming yet. It just isn't fair. "Why should anyone hear the Gospel twice before everyone has heard it once?" You know as well as I do, that not one individual in that entire company of five thousand men, besides women and children, got a second helping until everyone had had a first helping.

There was an absolutely equal distribution of the food. With but few exceptions there has never been an equal distribution since. Some churches do not even go fifty-fifty. They do not send as much to the foreign field as they spend on themselves.

I have never known a minister to have any trouble with the back rows. All his trouble comes from the front rows. Those in the front rows are over-fed and they develop spiritual indigestion. They tell him how much to feed them; when to feed them; when to stop feeding them; how long to feed them; what kind of food to give them, etc. etc., and if he doesn't do it, they complain and find fault. If a minister had any sense, he would leave the front rows for a while and let them get hungry for once in their lives and go to the back rows, and then when he returned they would be ready to accept his ministry and there would be no murmuring or complaining.

My friends, I have been with the back rows. I have seen the countless millions in those back rows famishing for the Bread of Life. Is it right? Should we be concentrating on the front rows? Ought we not rather to be training the front rows to share what they have with the back rows, and thus reach *them* with the Gospel, those for whom nothing has been prepared?

Do you know that the greatest thing a church can do for itself is to send its pastor to one of the foreign mission fields of earth? There is no vacation like it. He will come back a new man; for no one can see the need with his own eyes and ever be the same again. It will do something to him. He will have something to talk about. He will be worth infinitely more to the church than he ever was before.

DR. DUFF'S APPEAL

Dr. Alexander Duff, that great veteran missionary to India, returned to Scotland to die, and as he stood before the General Assembly of the Presbyterian Church, he made his appeal, but there was no response. In the midst of his appeal he fainted and was carried off the platform. The doctor bent over him and examined his heart. Presently he opened his eyes.

"Where am I?" he cried. "Where am I?"

"Lie still," said the doctor. "You have had a heart attack. Lie still."

"But," exclaimed Dr. Duff, "I haven't finished my appeal. Take me back. Take me back. I must finish my appeal."

"Lie still," said the doctor again. "You will go back at the peril of your life."

But, in spite of the protests of the physician, the old warrior struggled to his feet, and, with the doctor on one side and the Moderator of the Assembly on the other side, he again mounted the steps of the pulpit platform, and, as he did so, the entire Assembly rose to do him honour. Then, when they were seated, he continued his appeal, and this is what he said:

"When Queen Victoria calls for volunteers for India, hundreds of young men respond, but, when King Jesus calls, no one goes."

Then he paused. There was silence. Again he spoke:

"Is it true," he asked, "that the fathers and mothers of Scotland have no more sons to give for India?"

Again he paused. Still there was silence.

"Very well," he concluded, "then, aged though I am, I'll go back to India. I can lie down on the banks of the Ganges and I can die and thereby I can let the people of India know that there was one man in Scotland who loved them enough to give his life for them."

In a moment young men all over the Assembly sprang to their feet, crying, "I'll go! I'll go!" And after the old white-haired warrior had been laid to rest, these young men, having graduated, found their way to dark benighted India, there to labour as his substitutes for the Lord Jesus Christ.

My friend, will you go? Has God spoken to you? Have you heard His call? Will you not answer, "Lord, here am I, send me"? And if you cannot go, will you not send a substitute? It is for you to decide.

Why should anyone hear the Gospel twice before everyone has heard it once?

CHAPTER IV

WILL CHRIST RETURN TO EARTH BEFORE THE WORLD HAS BEEN EVANGELIZED?

IF YOU will turn to the Gospel according to Mark, the thirteenth chapter and the tenth verse, you will find these words: "The Gospel must first be published among all nations." Then if you will turn to the Gospel of Matthew, the twenty-fourth chapter and the fourteenth verse, you will find the same statement, but with something added. It reads like this: "This Gospel of the kingdom shall be preached among all nations and then shall the End come."

Before I comment on these passages I want to clarify my subject. I am not asking the question, "Will Christ return to the air?" In fact, I am not speaking about the rapture at all. My question is: "Will Christ return to earth? Will He come to establish His kingdom and reign? Will He return to put an end to this Age and usher in the next? Will He return to earth before the world has been evangelized?"

Note also, if you will, that I am not asking if He will return to earth before the world has been Christianized. The word I have used is "evangelized," and there is a world of difference between Christianization and evangelization. To understand the message, therefore, you must understand the subject: "Will Christ return to earth before the world has been evangelized?"

When I first read the passages to which I have drawn your attention, and especially the one in Mark, I was puzzled. Why, I asked myself, did Jesus use the word "first"? Why did He not just say, "The Gospel must be published among all nations"? That would have made sense. That I could have understood. But that is not what He said.

He interjected the word "first." He stated that the Gospel must *first* be published among all nations. What did He mean? Why did He use the word "first"?

GOD'S PLAN

If you will read the entire chapter, you will discover that it has to do with the End-time of this present dispensation and the ushering in of the Golden Age. But as He relates the events, one by one, suddenly He pauses and He says this: "But first, before these things can come to pass; before the Age can end and the new Age be born, first, this Gospel must be published among all nations." In Matthew's Gospel you have these words added: "Then shall the end come." That makes it clear. The meaning cannot be mistaken. The Age will end when the world has been evangelized.

In other words, before Jesus Christ will return to earth to reign in millennial splendour, power, and glory, His Gospel must be proclaimed to every tribe, tongue, and nation. There must be some in Heaven from every race, according to Revelation; hence, our greatest obligation is to give His Gospel to all mankind. Acts 1:8 says it will be done.

Matthew, I know, speaks of the Gospel of the kingdom. I am preaching both the Gospel of the grace of God *and* the Gospel of the kingdom, constantly. The Gospel of the grace of God is the Good News that Jesus died for sinners. The Gospel of the kingdom is the Good News that Jesus is coming back to reign. Both messages must be proclaimed; and whether it is the Gospel of the grace of God or the Gospel of the kingdom, it makes no difference. In both cases, it is the Gospel, the Good News. And it must be published before the end comes.

Oh, that our statesmen knew the programme! They are trying to get rid of war and bloodshed, to abolish poverty and sickness; and, as far as possible, to eliminate death. They hold their Peace Conferences; they sign their pacts; they spend their money for relief; and they think they can accomplish their purpose. How little they know!

If they knew God's plan they would organize and send out the largest army of missionaries they could muster, tens of thousands of them. They would place their radio stations at the disposal of Christian agencies. They would use their newspapers for the publishing of the Gospel; and in a few years they would succeed in reaching every man, woman, and child; and the whole world would be evangelized.

Then Christ would be here. He would set up His kingdom. War would be no more; sickness and poverty would be gone; seldom would there be a death for man would live his allotted life. The millennium would be established and man's rule ended. Christ would take over the reins of government and rule this world in righteousness. There would be prosperity never known before.

But the rulers do not know and the Church struggles on. The world still waits to be evangelized and Christ does not return. When, oh when, will we see God's plan? How long must He wait before we get down to business and do the job?

A Dangerous Theory

But I know what some are saying. I hear it everywhere. They are saying: "This is not the task of the Church at all, the Jews are to do it; we should leave it for them after we have been raptured away."

I know of no theory that can do more to cut the nerve of missionary endeavour. Moreover, I know of no definite statement in the entire Bible that would lead me to believe, for one single moment, that the Jews are to evangelize the world during the days of the great tribulation, as some people seem to think. Were I to believe that I would fold my arms and do nothing.

Do you mean to say that after the Holy Spirit has gone, and we are told that He is to go when the Church goes, do you mean to say that the Jews can accomplish more in some seven years or less, without the help of the Holy Spirit, in the midst of persecution and martyrdom, than we have been able to accomplish in nearly two thousand years, with the Holy Spirit's aid, when it has been easy to be a Christian? Preposterous! Impossible!

Furthermore, if nothing is to be done until the Church has been raptured, then only that one generation, the generation that will be living during the tribulation, will ever be evangelized. Are you willing then that every other generation should perish? Have you no concern for your own generation? Are we going to allow this generation to be lost and be satisfied if the last generation only, is evangelized? Paul's burden was for the first generation of the Christian era.

Even if you are right, still I am going to do all I can, because the job has to be done sometime. Everyone agrees on that. Well then, the more I can do now the less the Jews will have to do then. But if you are wrong, what a tragedy! You will have failed to do your part to evangelize the world and God will hold you responsible. I believe it must be done now.

ONE THING ONLY

When Jesus left His disciples, nearly two thousand years ago now, He gave them but one task; namely, world evangelization. I can imagine Him talking to them something like this: "I am going to leave you and I will be gone for a long time. While I am absent, I want you to do just one thing. Give this Gospel of Mine to the entire world. See that every nation, tongue, and tribe hears it."

Those were His instructions. That was the one thing He told them to do, and they understood Him perfectly. But what has the Church done during the years He has been absent? Have we carried out His orders? Have we obeyed Him?

As a matter of fact, we have done everything else except the one and only thing He told us to do. Jesus never told us to build colleges, universities, and seminaries, but we have done it. He never told us to erect hospitals and asylums and homes for the aged. He never told us to build churches or to organize Sunday Schools and Youth for Christ Rallies, but we have done it. And we ought to have done it, for it is all important and worthwhile.

But the one and only thing that He did tell us to do, is the one and only thing that we have left undone. We have not given His Gospel to the entire world. We have not carried out His orders.

What would a man say who had called a plumber to fix his water taps, if he should come home and find him painting the side of his house? What could he say? Would he not expect him to do what he had told him to do? Could the man satisfy him by stating that he thought the house needed painting? Of course not. Orders must be obeyed.

More than nineteen hundred years ago the Lord Jesus Christ ascended to His Father's throne and sat down on His right hand. But He has a throne of His own, the throne of His father David, and He is the legal successor. Whoever heard of a king, who had a throne of his own, who would be satisfied to occupy another king's throne?

Christ wants to return. He longs to reign. It is His right. Then why does He wait? He is waiting for you and me to complete the task. He is waiting for us to do what He has told us to do. Many a time He must say to Himself as He sits there, "How long, I wonder, are they going to keep Me waiting? When will they let Me come back? How soon can I return to earth to sit on My throne and reign?"

THE WHOLE ESTATE

Here is an estate. The master tells his servants that he is leaving, but that he will be returning. And while he is gone, they are to bring the entire estate under cultivation.

They begin working around the house. They beautify the gardens and flower-beds. Next year the weeds grow and again they go to work, keeping the lawns in perfect condition. Presently one of them remembers his master's orders. "I must go," he exclaims. "Our master told us to bring the entire estate under cultivation." And he prepares to leave. "But," they cry, "we cannot spare you. See how fast the weeds grow. We need you here." In spite of their protests, however, he leaves and begins working in a far corner of the estate.

Later on, two others remember their lord's orders and in spite of objections they, too, go and cultivate another part of the estate.

At last their master returns. He is pleased as he looks at the flower-beds and gardens and the lawns around his house. But before rewarding his servants, he decides to explore the rest of the estate and, as he does so, his heart sinks for he sees nothing but wilderness and marsh, and he realizes that there has not even been an attempt made to cultivate it.

Finally he comes to the one man working all by himself in a distant part of the estate and he rewards him richly. He discovers the two in still another part and likewise rewards them. Then he returns to headquarters where his servants are waiting and expecting a reward; but his face indicates displeasure.

"Have we not been faithful?" they exclaim. "Look at these flower-beds and gardens. Look at these lawns. Are they not beautiful? And have we not worked hard?"

"Yes," he replies, "you have done your best. You have been faithful. You have laboured diligently."

"Well then," they cry, "why are you disappointed? Are we not entitled to a reward?"

"There is one thing you have forgotten," he replies; "you have forgotten my orders. I did not tell you to work the same gardens and lawns again and again, year after year. I told you to bring the entire estate under cultivation, to cultivate it at least once. That you did not do; in fact, you did not even attempt to cultivate it, and when your companions insisted upon going and doing their part, you objected. No, there is no reward."

Many a one, I am afraid, is going to be disappointed. You may be that one. You may have won many souls in your town. You may have been most faithful to your church; but what have you done for those in heathen darkness? Did you ever think of going yourself? Have you ever given your money that someone else might go? Have you prayed? What part have you had in the evangelization of the world? Have you obeyed orders? Have you done what you could to bring the entire estate under cultivation? Or have you been satisfied to work in your own community and let the rest of the world perish?

If you want to hear Him say, "Well done, good and faithful servant, enter thou into the joy of thy Lord," and if you want to receive the promised reward, the diadem or the crown, you had better get busy and do what you can to publish His Gospel among all nations, or you will be a missing Christian in the day of rewards.

Go then and do your part. Either go yourself or send someone else. There is something that you can do, and the time is short. It was the whole estate that had to be cultivated, and it is the whole world that must be evangelized. "Go ye therefore into all the world, and preach the Gospel to every creature." For remember, "The Gospel must first be published among all nations, and then shall the end come."

This then is His answer to their question. "What shall be THE sign of Thy coming, and of the end of the age?" That was what they wanted to know—THE sign preceding and indicating the end. His answer to their question in verse 3 of Matthew 24 is found in verse 14. Here it is: "This Gospel shall be preached *in all the world*, for a witness unto *all nations*; and THEN shall the end come." All His other predictions indicate the *approaching* end; this one, THE end. Hence the word "first" in Mark 13:10. It is God's programme: first world evangelization; then, the reign of Christ. He will return to establish His kingdom when all nations have heard the Gospel. Let us, then, to our task; and may we never rest until our work is done.

CHAPTER V

ARE WE WINNING THE BATTLE AGAINST HEATHENISM?

LET US turn to Romans, the tenth chapter, verses thirteen to fifteen. They read as follows: "For whosoever shall call upon the name of the Lord shall be saved. How then shall they call on Him in whom they have not believed? And how shall they believe in Him of whom they have not heard? And how shall they hear without a preacher? And how shall they preach, except they be sent? As it is written, How beautiful are the feet of them that preach the Gospel of peace, and bring glad tidings of good things!"

Here you have the four "hows" of God's Word. First there is the promise, "call" and "be saved." But to call, they must believe. To believe, they must hear. To hear, someone must preach. To preach, he must be sent. Thus God puts the responsibility on us. If we send, the missionary can preach. If he preaches, the heathen can hear and believe. If he believes, he can call. If he calls, he will be saved. But it starts with us. We must first of all *send*.

THE MOST IMPORTANT WORK

What, then, is the most important work of the hour? *It is to carry out our Lord's last orders. It is to give His Gospel to the unreached tribes and peoples of the world.* That, my friends, is more important than anything else. "Go ye into all the world, and preach the Gospel to every creature" (Mark 16:15).

By this, and this alone, we must judge all spirituality, all Bible knowledge, all doctrinal and theological discussions. If we are truly spiritual, if we are real Bible students, if our

46

doctrines are scriptural, we will put world evangelism first; we will give, and give liberally, to missions. All our Bible knowledge, all our spirituality, all our doctrinal standards are nothing but make-believe, unless we are putting first things first.

Let those who do not have the vision, those who do not know God's programme, let them give to the many worthy causes here at home; but let those of us who have heard God's call, let us concentrate on pioneer work in the regions beyond. Let us put our money into one thing and one thing only, that of reaching the unevangelized tribes with the Gospel of Jesus Christ.

There are those without a vision, who are moved by appeals and give a little here and a little there, and have but little to show for it, whereas they could put all they give back of the most important work of the hour and see a whole new tribe or a whole new country evangelized. There are men who could have the untold joy of supporting fifty or a hundred missionaries in pioneer territory, who are today giving to a hundred and one nearby enterprises, to which thousands who do not have the God-given vision of world evangelism are glad to contribute. The home work will never lack.

We have but one great task and God's Word, "his blood will I require at thine hand," will apply to us if we withhold the Gospel. If the King is to reign, we must finish the task. He is counting on us. How long, I wonder, are we going to keep Him waiting? We should lay everything else aside and concentrate on this one great objective, the completion of the evangelization of the world in our own generation.

Oh, my friend, let me urge you in the few short years that remain, to turn from everything else, to bend every effort to send out the Gospel, for this is the one and only task that Jesus left His Church to do. This, and this alone, is the most important work of the hour. Are we doing it? How are we getting along? What progress are we making? Are we winning the battle against heathenism? Let us see.

LANGUAGES AND TRIBES STILL UNREACHED

Do you know how many languages there are in this world of ours? Let me tell you. At the present time there are at least 2,974 major languages. Do you know how many of these languages have the Word of God, or any portion of it? Up to the present time only 1,185. How many, then, does that leave without a single portion of God's Book? It leaves 1,789. Think of it, if you will. After nearly two thousand years of missionary work and world-wide evangelism, there are still 1,789 languages into which the Word of God has never yet been translated. And what does God say? "Faith cometh by hearing, and hearing by the Word of God." "How shall they believe except they hear?" But how can they hear if they do not have God's Word?

It has been found that there are still over 2,000 tribes without the Gospel. Moreover, these tribes have been located. We know where they are. I want you to think of them, if you will, as I mention them, and remember, no missionary is working among them and none of them have the Word of God. As a matter of fact, they have never even heard the name of Jesus.

There are 626 tribes in New Guinea, 521 in the South Sea Islands, 350 in Africa, 300 in South America, 200 in Australia (Aborigines), 100 in India, 60 in Indo-China and 60 in the Philippines. Hence, at least 2,000 tribes are still waiting in darkness and midnight gloom for the Gospel of Jesus Christ.

In Brazil alone there are 1,500,000 pure blood Indians and more than 100 tribes. Bolivia has almost 1,000,000 pure blood Indians. Peru has an Indian population of 2,500,000. In Colombia there are 100,000 Indians, mostly in a savage and primitive condition. There are also 500,000 highland Indians in a semi-civilized state.

But how are they to be reached? Only by the young people of our churches, our Bible Schools and our Seminaries. It is the young who can go. Mission Boards everywhere are pleading for workers.

That is why I toured Great Britain and appealed to the young people there until 1,200 of them responded. That is why I have gone all over the United States and Canada. "The labourers are few." We must have more. That is why I am giving myself first and foremost to missionary work. The world must be evangelized. Our only hope is in the young people. Unless they go, the job will never be done for no one else can do it. God is calling the young. The youth of our country must respond.

Let us remember that practically all the disciples were young men. Jesus chose them in their youth. They had their lives before them and they lived them for God. May we, too, accept the challenge. May we give our best. God had an only Son and He made Him a missionary. Can we do less?

There are many who would go if they could be pioneers. They have read the life stories of men like Livingstone, Moffat, Carey, Judson, etc. My friends, may I say that the Missionary Societies are calling for thousands of pioneers right now, for there are still two thousand tribes to be evangelized. Why not concentrate on the unoccupied areas? Why not be a trail-blazer?

When I was in Sumatra I heard of a town to which no one had gone, and I penetrated back through the jungles until I reached it. Never will I forget the thrill that was mine as I crossed the threshold of that town, realizing that I was in all probability the first messenger of the Cross to have done so. If I were a young man today, I would not want to go to a field where others had laboured, except to become "oriented." I would ask, as Livingstone did, to be sent to new fields, for I would want to be the first to reduce the language to writing, translate portions of the Bible, and give the people the Gospel. I, too, would be a pioneer.

Why waste your life here in America or Great Britain? Why settle down to the humdrum and the monotony of making money? Why not get a vision? You can go where no one else has gone. You can invest your life in something really worthwhile. If you stay here, you will be treading on someone else's toes. If you go out there, you will have plenty of elbow room. Why not live a life really worthwhile? You, too, can be a pioneer.

Oh, I know what you are saying. I have heard it said again and again. You are quoting Acts 1:8; but you are not quoting it right. This is the way you quote it: "Ye shall be witnesses unto Me *first* in Jerusalem, *then* in Judea; after that in Samaria, and *last* of all, to the uttermost part of the earth." But that is not what it says. Let me quote it for you now: "Ye shall be witnesses unto me *both* in Jerusalem, *and* in all Judea, *and* in Samaria, *and* unto the uttermost part of the earth." It is not, "first," but "both." And what does the word *both* mean? It means at one and the same time, does it not? In other words, we are to evangelize Jerusalem, and, at one and the same time, Judea, and Samaria, and the uttermost part of the earth. We are not to wait until we have completed the work here, before going there. We are to work both fields; the home and the foreign, together.

HOME OR FOREIGN—WHICH?

Do you realize that all can hear here, if they want to? Since the advent of radio, all anyone has to do, even in the most remote place, is to tune in on a Gospel programme and listen to the message. But I have been in countries where there are millions of people and no radio, either sending stations or receiving sets; and where the people could not hear if they wanted to. Why then be so concerned for those in the homeland, who for the most part are not interested, and so little concerned for those in distant lands who would be interested if they had a chance?

Think, if you will, of the hundreds upon hundreds of different organizations here at home for the propagation of the Gospel. Then think of the few in foreign lands. It just doesn't seem fair. We have concentrated on the home work and have forgotten those for whom nothing has been prepared. What would you do if you should see ten men lifting a log and if nine were on one end and one on the other? Where would you help? Why on the end where the one was lifting, would you not? Need I say more? It is the foreign field that needs our help most.

This then is the most important work of the hour—to finish the unfinished task. "How shall they hear without a preacher (or a missionary), and how shall they preach except they be sent?" Are we winning the battle against heathenism? It is for you to say.

CHAPTER VI

WHY HAS THE CHURCH FAILED TO EVANGELIZE THE WORLD?

TURN, IF you will, to the Word of God as it is found in John's Gospel, chapter four, verse thirty-five. "Say not ye, There are yet four months, and then cometh harvest? Behold, I say unto you, Lift up your eyes, and look on the fields; for they are white already to harvest." My friends, my heart burns within me whenever I read these words. How true they are even today!

Nearly 2,000 years have now gone by since Jesus Christ told us to evangelize the world and yet there are still two thousand tribes without the Gospel, while multiplied millions in countries like China and India—yellow, black and brown—have never once heard of Christ. At least sixty-five per cent of earth's three billion inhabitants are still unevangelized.

God's commands are always accompanied by His enablements. We could have done it. He would not have mocked us by asking us to do the impossible. "The Gospel *MUST* be published among *ALL* nations." Why then has it not been done?

FIRST—BECAUSE OF THE ENEMIES OF THE GOSPEL

We are confronted today with enemies we have never faced before, and sometimes we wonder if we can overcome them. There are three especially with which we must contend. I refer to Nationalism, False Religions, and Communism.

Nationalism is manifesting itself in almost every country and it is making missionary work increasingly difficult. Its slogan is "Africa for the African, India for the Indian, China for the Chinaman, etc.," and it is determined to drive the white man out. Foreigners are looked upon with suspicion and even the missionary is no longer welcome.

False Religions have always been the enemies of the Gospel, especially Mohammedanism and Roman Catholicism. Neither believes in freedom of any kind. Where Roman Catholicism is weak, it cries out for tolerance and freedom; as soon as it becomes strong, it becomes totalitarian and freedom is unknown. Christians are persecuted, tortured and martyred wherever it holds sway. It knows no mercy and shows none. Protestantism is the only religion that believes in and practices freedom.

Communism is the most diabolical weapon ever devised by Satanic ingenuity. It has spread faster than any other ism and it is attacking Christianity in every country. It boasts of a million followers in South America alone. This demon-inspired, atheistic movement will never compromise. Its Iron Curtain cuts off all intercourse with the outside world and conceals the Red Terror within. It murdered John and Betty Stam and, whenever possible, it will silence anyone who attempts to preach the Gospel.

These then, are the enemies of the Gospel. But in spite of all opposition we must press forward, taking our orders from God alone. "Behold, I give unto you authority over all the power of the enemy" (Luke 10:19). There is power in the Gospel to overcome every foe and to evangelize the world. "The Gospel . . . is the power of God unto salvation to everyone that believeth" (Rom. 1:16).

SECOND—Because of Our Emphasis on Education

Now I believe in education. Schools are necessary. There are those who must make up for their deficiencies somehow. But there are men with natural talents, men like Moody, Philpott, and Gipsy Smith, who will succeed either with or without an education. Today we worship diplomas, we glory in degrees. Yet there are some men who cannot make good even with a degree.

Fransom sent Hudson Taylor one hundred new missionaries. They had little or no education, and when Taylor saw them he wrote Fransom reprimanding him for sending them. Two years later he wrote again. He had seen their work. They had made good, for they were Spirit-filled men, and God had given them the language and blessed their efforts, and he wanted more like them.

THIRD—Because of the Many Closed Doors

But what about the open doors? Why not enter them? Do we not spend too much time praying for the closed doors to open, when there are so many doors still open, waiting to be entered? Paul, you remember, turned from the closed doors, one after the other, and entered those that were open. There are open doors everywhere. Let us enter them and leave God to open the closed ones in His own good time. He knows where and when He wants us to work, and He will make it plain.

FOURTH—Because We have Not Sent Out a Sufficient Number of Missionaries

The problem is still one of labourers. In China there are vast harvest fields and they have to be reaped by hand; yet they are always reaped. Why? Because every man, woman, boy and girl, able to carry a sickle, goes to work; hence, there are labourers in abundance.

Our Lord recognized that problem. He said, "The harvest is plenteous but the labourers are few. Pray ye therefore the Lord of the harvest, that He will send forth labourers into His harvest" (Matt. 9:37, 38). If we had a sufficient number of labourers, the job could be done, but we have always been short-handed. Today, with our increased population, the labourers are as few, in comparison, as they were in the days of Jesus. That is why we are continually appealing to young men and women to volunteer for missionary service. We must get more labourers.

FIFTH—BECAUSE WE HAVE NOT FOLLOWED THE PAULINE METHODS

In 2 Timothy 2:2, we have the Pauline method stated: "And the things that thou hast heard of me among many witnesses, the same commit thou to faithful men, who shall be able to teach others also." Paul's method was to teach others, and then in turn they were to teach still others; thus workers were provided, workers trained and equipped.

Now the best way to do that today is by means of Bible Schools. The first thing we should do when we get to a foreign field is to establish a Bible School, train the workers that are available, as soon as they have been won to Christ, and then send them out as evangelists to their own people. The native himself is the key to the situation. The foreign missionary can never hope to evangelize the world. The day will never come when we will be able to put a missionary from the homeland in every village, town, and city throughout the world.

Jesus, you remember, trained the twelve; then the seventy. Paul never became a pastor. He won converts, ordained elders, and passed on. He placed the churches under native leadership and made them self-supporting from the very first. They were living organisms. Living organisms will grow.

In Acts, chapter 19, verses eight to ten and verses eighteen to twenty, we have a marvellous example of the Pauline method. In two short years, we are told, all those in Asia heard the Gospel. Asia covered a territory of approximately 50,000 square miles. There was a mighty revival. Books belonging to various false cults were burned publicly; books costing thousands of dollars, so great was the upheaval.

How did it happen? Paul took charge of a school and every day he taught. Most certainly he did not, himself, travel throughout Asia and evangelize the country. So far as the record goes, he stayed in one place, but he taught others;

then they in turn went everywhere preaching the Gospel, with the results described in the nineteenth chapter. Wherever he went, he "preached and *taught*" (Acts 14:21). That method cannot be improved upon. It will work everywhere.

The West Indies Mission has proved it. They started in Cuba with a Bible School. Not a church, mark you, but a Bible School. Then they went to Haiti and established another. Later they put one in the Dominican Republic and another in Jamaica. Now they are starting a fifth in one of the French islands. What has been the result? The students in hundreds have gone from their Bible Schools throughout the length and breadth of the islands of the West Indies, and more than 80,000 have been won to the Lord Jesus Christ.

The old method had been followed for decades. Churches had been built in the larger towns and cities, but the country districts, where most of the people lived, were left untouched and unevangelized. The West Indies Mission went in. The Pauline method was adopted. Now annual conferences number upwards of 7,000 or more; so great has grown the Word of God and multiplied.

In Ethiopia the missionaries had made but little headway. There were only a handful of believers when I was there. Then the natives themselves took over and during the Italian occupation, in spite of imprisonment, floggings, and martyrdom, 20,000 were brought to Christ, and that without the help of a single missionary. Today there are 50,000 Christians and 300 native churches. What a miracle! That is the ideal way. It is the only method that really succeeds.

Such a method cuts down expenses. The natives can live cheaper. No furloughs are necessary. They can be supported by their own churches. Foreign funds are not required. All we have to do is to support the missionary and his work, and leave it to the natives to do the rest. The work then becomes self-supporting, self-governing, and self-propagating. That is the scriptural way. The Pauline method cannot be improved upon.

SIXTH—BECAUSE WE HAVE NOT BEEN CONVINCED THAT THE HEATHEN ARE LOST

If they are not lost until they hear, then we had better leave them as they are. If only those who definitely reject Christ are to perish, we should never tell them about Him. Better to leave them in their ignorance than to bring them under condemnation. But the teaching of the whole Bible is that men without Christ are lost and that their only hope of salvation is in the Gospel.

Paul speaks of the heathen world in these words: "dead in trespasses and sins, children of wrath, having no hope and without God" (Eph. 2:1, 3, 12). Could language be plainer? That is their condition. They are irretrievably and eternally lost.

Now there are two passages that settle it once and for all. The first is Acts 4:12, where it reads: "Neither is there salvation in any other; for there is none other name under heaven given among men, whereby we must be saved." None of their gods, none of their religions can avail. The names of Mohammed, Confucius, Buddha, and all others, are ruled out. Christ, and Christ alone, can save.

The second statement is found in John 14:6, where Jesus says: "No man cometh unto the Father but by *ME*." No other way to God. Christ or damnation. "I am the Way," He declares. No one else can be. No one else is. If the heathen are not lost, then these two verses do not mean what they say.

But you say it is unjust. You find fault with God. You think a God of love would not and could not permit it. Does God owe us salvation? If so, then it is not of grace at all. He is simply paying a debt. But we deserve nothing. It is all of grace.

My friend, you can rest on one great statement and it is this: "Shall not the Judge of all the earth do right?" I do not know what He will do, but I do know that He will be absolutely just. He will do right. I can leave it in His hands. And when at last I find out what He has done, I will be completely satisfied, for I will say, "He did right. He did what I would have done had I been in His place." We will agree with the verdict of the angel: "True and righteous are Thy judgments" (Rev. 16:7).

We all want to do the will of God, and we know that there is nothing nearer to His heart than the evangelization of the world. If we have failed in the past, that is no reason why we should fail in the future. Let us then to our task. Let us work while it is called today. The world must be evangelized. Why not complete it in our own generation?

CHAPTER VII

HOW GOD TAUGHT ME TO GIVE TO MISSIONS

"GIVE according to your income lest God make your income according to your giving."—*Peter Marshall.*
I had been pastor of a large Presbyterian Church in the City of Toronto. Presently one day I resigned and became pastor of a church that knew how to give in a way I had never known.

I commenced my pastorate on the first Sunday of January. The church was holding its Annual Missionary Convention. Now I knew nothing about a convention. I had never seen one in all my life, so I just sat on the platform and watched.

The ushers were going up and down the aisles giving out envelopes. Presently, to my amazement, one of the ushers had the audacity to walk right up the aisle and hand me— the pastor—one of the envelopes. I sat there holding it in my hand. Never will I forget that moment. I can still remember it as though it were yesterday.

As I held it I read it: "In dependence upon God I will endeavour to give toward the Missionary Work of the Church $ . . . each month for a year." I had never read such a statement before. I did not know that that morning God was going to deal with me and teach me a lesson that I was never to forget, and that I in turn was to teach scores of other churches all over the country in the years to come.

At first I started to pray. I said, "Lord, I can't do anything. You know I have nothing. I haven't a cent in the Bank. I haven't anything in my pocket. This church only pays me $25.00 a week. I have a wife and child to keep. We are trying to buy our home, and everything is sky-high in price." All that was true. The First World War was on.

"I know that," the Lord said. "I know you are only getting $25.00 a week. I know you have nothing in your pocket and nothing in the Bank."

"Well, then," I continued, "that settles it. I have nothing to give."

It was then the Lord spoke. I will never forget it.

"I am not asking you for what you have," He said.

"You are not asking me for what I have, Lord? Then what are you asking?" I replied.

"I am asking you for a Faith Offering. How much can you trust Me for?"

"Oh, Lord," I exclaimed, "that's different. How much can I trust Thee for?"

Now, of course, I knew nothing at all about a Faith-Promise Offering. I had never given such an offering in my life. But I knew the Lord was speaking. I thought He might say $5.00 or perhaps even $10.00. Once in my life I had given $5.00 to missions. Once I had given $2.00. But never more. I almost trembled as I waited for the answer.

Presently it came. Now I am not going to ask you to believe that God spoke to me in an audible voice, but He might just as well have done so. I was scarcely conscious of the congregation, as I sat there with my eyes closed, listening to the Voice of God. God was dealing with me that morning, though I did not realize it at the time.

"How much can I give?" I asked.

"Fifty dollars."

"Fifty dollars!" I exclaimed. "Why, Lord, that's two weeks' salary. How can I ever get $50.00?"

But again the Lord spoke and it was still the same amount. It was just as clear to me as though He had spoken in an audible voice.

I can still remember how my hand trembled as I took my pencil, signed my name and address and wrote in the amount of $50.00.

Now, how I ever paid it I don't know to this day. All I know is that every month I had to pray for $4.00, and every month God sent it in some miraculous way. At the end of the year I had paid the entire amount—$50.00.

But this is what I want to make clear. I received such a blessing, there came to my heart such a fulness of the Spirit, it was such a thrill, that as I paid the final amount, I realized that it had been one of the greatest experiences of my life.

So great was the spiritual blessing that had come to me because I had given a Faith-Promise Offering, I had trusted God for a certain amount, I had given in a scriptural way, that the next year at the Convention, I doubled the amount and gave $100.00. Then, at another Convention, I doubled the amount again and gave $200.00. Then the church raised my salary and I received more than I had given. You see, you can't beat God giving. At still another Convention I doubled it once more and gave $400.00. Then, at another Convention still, I doubled it once again and made it $800.00.

From that day to this I have been increasing the amount and sending on thousands upon thousands of dollars to the Bank of Heaven year by year. If I had waited until I had it, I never would have given it, because I never would have had it. But I gave it when I didn't have it. I gave a Faith-Promise Offering and God honoured it.

A Faith-Promise Offering

Paul, you remember, got the church to promise a certain amount and then he would give them a year to pay it. As the year drew to a close, he would send Titus, or someone else, to remind the church of the promise that had been made, so that he would not be ashamed when he arrived. Then, at the end of the year, he came and collected it. Therefore, a Faith-Promise Offering is a Pauline offering and God blesses it. (See chapters 8 and 9 of 2 Cor. in Living Letters.)

Have you ever in your life given a Faith-Promise Offering, or have you only given a cash offering? It doesn't require any faith to give a cash offering. If I have a dollar in my pocket, all I have to do is to tell my hand to go into my pocket, find the dollar, take it out and put it on the plate. I don't have to pray for it. I just give it.

But with a Faith-Promise Offering it is entirely different. I have to pray about it and ask God how much He would have me give, and then trust Him for it, and month by month, go to Him in prayer and ask Him for the amount promised, and wait upon Him until it comes in. That is the offering that brings the blessing.

That is the only kind of an offering I have taken up for missions in all these years, nearly half a century now—a Faith-Promise Offering. I would never go back to the cash offering for anything. With a cash offering I could only get a very little, but with a Faith-Promise Offering I can get much. In our Annual Missionary Convention we never get more than $7,000.00 in cash, but we get over $400,000 in Faith Promises.

There is many a church that will not give a Faith-Promise Offering. They are not interested in scriptural giving. They will not obligate themselves for the definite support of their missionaries. They simply divide whatever cash comes in, between various missionary societies. They don't have to trust God for anything. If it comes in, they give it. But since there is no need to exercise faith, therefore, there is no burden, no responsibility. I do not like that kind of giving. I believe that every individual church should obligate itself in faith before God for a certain definite amount, and pray until that amount has been received.

I do not believe in pledges. I have never taken up a pledge offering in my life. What is the difference, you ask, between a pledge offering and a Faith-Promise Offering? All the difference in the world. A pledge offering is between you and a church, between you and a missionary society, and some day the deacons may come along and try to collect it, or you may receive a letter asking for it. In other words, you can be held responsible for a pledge offering.

A Faith-Promise Offering, on the other hand, is between you and God. No one will ever ask you for it. No official will ever call on you to collect it. No one will ever send you a letter reminding you of it. It is a promise made by you to God, and to God alone. If you are unable to pay it, all you have to do is to tell God. Give Him your excuse, and if He accepts it, you do not have to pay it.

I have gone to many a church that has been opposed to a pledge offering, but as soon as I have explained the nature of a Faith-Promise Offering, all opposition has disappeared, and those who have been most antagonistic to a pledge of any kind, have been perfectly willing to accept the plan of a Faith-Promise Offering, and God has accomplished wonders. I believe we could get all the missionary money we need if we would take up Faith-Promise Offerings in all our churches.

How can the church know how many missionaries to accept for support unless you make a Faith-Promise? You are not behind the missionary policy of your church if you do not co-operate in the programme. The only men who ever become officers in The Peoples Church are those who are backing the world-wide missionary work of the church.

The Man in Minneapolis

I was holding an evangelistic campaign in Minneapolis in the great church of which the Rev. Paul Rees was pastor. Large crowds gathered night after night, sometimes capacity audiences. Many souls were saved and there was much spiritual blessing.

At the close of one of my services, as I stood by the pulpit— after having pronounced the benediction—I saw a well-dressed business man approaching me.

"I owe everything I am and everything I have to you," were his words of greeting. I looked at him in amazement.

"You owe everything you are and everything you have to me?" I repeated. "What do you mean? I don't understand."

Briefly he told me his story, a story that I have never forgotten.

"I was in Toronto," he said, "your city, and I was out of work. I found myself in debt. It was in the days of the depression. I could not find anything to do. I kept sinking lower and lower, finding it impossible to get a job.

"At last," he continued, "my two daughters left me, then my wife left me, and finally I became an ordinary bum. I was so low that I could hardly reach up to touch bottom.

"One day I was walking along Bloor Street and as I passed The Peoples Church I heard singing. The doors were open and, having nothing else to do, I walked in and sat in a seat near the back of the church.

"You were holding one of those missionary conventions of yours and you were in the pulpit, but you were making some of the most amazing, some of the most nonsensical and foolish statements I had ever heard in my life. You were saying, 'Give, and it shall be given unto you. You can't beat God giving. God will be no man's debtor.'

"I listened," he said, "in utter amazement. There I was, down and out, with nothing, and you were stating that if I would give I would get. Just to see whether or not you were telling the truth, I took one of your envelopes from a passing usher and I filled it in, promising to give God a percentage of all He might give me in the days to come. That was easy, of course, because I had nothing.

"But then, to my amazement, things began to happen and happen fast. Within a few hours I had a job. When I got my first money I gave the percentage I had promised to God. A little later on I got a raise in pay, then I was able to give a larger amount. After a while I got another job with still better wages and then I gave more. It was working, and working wonderfully, so I kept on. Every week I faithfully gave God the percentage I had promised Him.

"In due time I got another suit of clothes. I was able to dress better. After a while my wife came back to me. Then my two daughters returned to me, and before many months had passed, I had paid every debt, for again my salary had been raised.

"To cut a long story short, I am now a prosperous business man, living in Minneapolis. We own our own home. My wife is with me and my two daughters. I have a bank account. I am not in debt. What you told me when I was down and out was absolutely true."

My friends, I have had that experience again and again. God will be no man's debtor. "Give, and it shall be given unto you." You can't beat God giving. "There is that scattereth, and yet increaseth; and there is that withholdeth more than is meet, but it tendeth to poverty. The liberal soul shall be made fat: and he that watereth shall be watered also himself" (Proverbs 11:24-25).

During the days of the depression, hundreds of men came to my office for a hand-out, or a shake-down for the night. Many a time I asked them this question: "When you were earning money, did you square with God? Did you give God that which belonged to Him?" Never once did I have that question answered in the affirmative. Every man who came for a hand-out had to admit that he had not squared with God in the years of prosperity.

You just cannot get away from it. It is one of the unchangeable laws of God. You square with God and God will square with you. You give to God in days of prosperity and God will give to you in days of depression. You withhold from God in days of prosperity and God will withhold from you in days of depression. If you faithfully give to God you will never find yourself in the bread-line. Just why it works like that I do not know, but I know it does.

THE SEA OF GALILEE AND THE DEAD SEA

When I was in Palestine, I travelled from Jerusalem down the Jericho Road. I passed the ruins of the ancient city of Jericho and went on to the Jordan River where Jesus was baptized. I wanted to swim across the Jordan at that point and I did so. Then I continued to the Dead Sea where I had another swim. Travelling north, I came at length to the Sea of Galilee and there, too, I indulged in a swim. As I stood on the shore, I thought of the difference between the two bodies of water; one, the Sea of Galilee, teeming with life, the other, the Dead Sea, stagnant and lifeless. "Why," I asked myself, "the difference?"

The Dead Sea takes in and takes in, but it never gives out; hence it is stagnant. The Sea of Galilee takes in but it also gives out; hence, it is filled with life; and its water is fresh.

There you have a perfect illustration of the missionary church and the church that is not interested in missions. The latter takes in but it uses everything on itself. It never gives out. Hence it is filled with all sorts of loathsome creatures like a stagnant pool—criticism, gossip, fault-finding, division, and strife, etc., etc. The missionary church takes in, but it also gives out. Hence it is alive and aggressive and God's blessing rests upon it.

The same is true of the individual. The one who keeps everything for himself and refuses to share it with others, becomes a stagnant pool—a Dead Sea, a blessing to no one. The one who invests in foreign missionary work, is living an abundant life. It is for us to decide whether our lives are to be symbolized by the Dead Sea or the Sea of Galilee.

Where are You Laying up Treasure?

You are either laying up treasure in Heaven or upon earth. Everything you have you must ultimately lose. Everything you invest in the souls of men, you will save. You are going to enter Heaven either a pauper, having sent nothing on ahead, or as one who is to receive an inheritance, made possible by contributions laid up while still upon earth.

It reminds me of a legend of a very wealthy woman and her coachman. She was expecting a mansion in Heaven, but she was led past the mansions to a little humble abode. Upon inquiring as to the owner of one of the mansions, she was told that her coachman was to live there. When she expressed amazement and disappointment, she was informed that he had been sending up materials all his lifetime by investing his money in the souls of men, especially in foreign lands; but that she had sent up almost nothing and that they had been forced to do the best they could with the material that they had.

Some of us are getting on in life. We have a very short time left in which to lay up treasure in Heaven. We had better start now or it will be too late. Everything we can send on ahead will await our arrival and we will receive it back, with dividends.

MONEY WILLED BRINGS NO REWARD

A great many people have an idea that they can "will" their money to missions and that they will then be entitled to a reward. Do you know that God never promises a reward for those who give away their money after they are dead and gone? Why should they be rewarded for that which they cannot help doing? God says very definitely that we are rewarded for "the deeds done in the body." In other words, we are rewarded only for what we do while we are still alive.

I want to know what my money is doing. I would not want to will it to missions and then have my relatives fight over it after I had gone, and lawyers get the most of it. I want to be sure that most of it goes now for the things in which I am interested. I want to give it, year by year, while I am still alive. Otherwise, I know there will be no reward.

THE MEANING OF SACRIFICE

Do you know the meaning of sacrifice? I will never forget a little girl by the name of Grace. She was saved in Dale Presbyterian Church when I was in my twenties. Her heart was in India. One day her mother told her she was going to buy her a new top coat. The one she was wearing was thread-bare. She had worn it for six years. But Grace begged her mother to give her the money, stating that she could wear her old coat for one more winter. Her mother did so and Grace sent it to her missionaries in India.

Before I left Dale, Grace was taken ill. On her death-bed she made her mother promise to sell all her clothes, such as they were, and send whatever she got to India. The mother, with tears in her eyes, promised. I would like to be standing somewhere near the throne when Grace gets her reward. Her heart was in India and her money followed her heart, regardless of the sacrifice. Do you, my friend, know anything about that kind of sacrifice?

THEY SHALL SHARE ALIKE

Suppose a child should fall into a well, who would get the reward for the child's rescue, the one who held the rope and lowered the other to the bottom, or both? God says they will share alike. The one who stands at the top and makes it possible for the other to go down into the well in order that the child might be rescued is just as much entitled to the reward as the one who goes down. You may not be able to go down; you may never see the foreign field, but you can hold the rope. You can make it possible for someone else to go. You can send a substitute; and if you do, if you give your money, your reward will be just as great as the reward of those who actually go.

Everyone must be in the bucket brigade. You may not be the one who throws the water on the fire at the end of the line; you may be somewhere in the centre passing the bucket. Or you may be dipping up the water. The question is, are you in the line? Do you belong to the bucket brigade? Are you doing something? Or are you merely a spectator? Our motto must be: "Every Christian a Missionary."

WHAT HAVE YOU DONE?

"God so loved that He gave." He gave His only Son. He gave Heaven's best. What have you given? Have you given yourself? Have you given your children? Have you given your prayers? Have you given your money? Have you given anything? What have you done for those in darkness and midnight gloom?

The martyrs gave their all; they gave their lives. I have preached in a Roman arena where fifty thousand Christians there and in other arenas, were thrown to the beasts or crucified; many of them made human torches, for their faith in Christ. I have stood on the sand once red with their blood. In the midst of the flames they cried out, "Christ is Victor!" They gave their all. What have you given?

How Much Shall I Give

1. If I refuse to give anything to missions this year, I practically cast a ballot in favour of the recall of every missionary.

2. If I give less than heretofore, I favour reduction of the missionary forces proportionate to my reduced contribution.

3. If I give the same as formerly, I favour holding the ground already won; but I oppose any forward movement. My song is "Hold the Fort," forgetting that the Lord never intended His army to take refuge in a fort. All His soldiers are commanded to "Go".

4. If I increase my offering beyond former years, then I favour an advance movement in the conquest of new territory for Christ.   — Quoted by permission

John Chinaman

John Chinaman was standing beside an Atheist. Said the Atheist to the Chinaman: "John Chinaman, what will be the first thing that you will do when you get to Heaven?"

Said John Chinaman: "When I first get to Heaven I am going to walk the golden street of Heaven until I find the Saviour, and then I will fall down and worship Him for having saved my soul."

"Fine!" sneered the Atheist. "And then, John Chinaman, what next will you do?"

"Then," said John Chinaman, "I will walk the streets of Heaven again until I find the missionary who came to my country with the Gospel. I will grasp his hand and thank him for his part in my salvation."

"What then will you do, John Chinaman?" inquired the Atheist.

"Then," responded John Chinaman, "I will search the streets of Heaven again until I find the man who gave the money to make it possible for the missionary to come, and I will grasp his hand, and thank him for his part in my salvation."

With that the Atheist turned on his heel and walked away.

My friend, will there be any John Chinaman from any country in the world, who will come up to you and thank you when you get to Heaven? Or will you be lonely in Heaven? Will no one recognize you except a few of your own relatives and friends?

I can think of no greater joy that could come to my heart in Heaven than to have multitudes of black people, multitudes of brown people, multitudes of yellow people, stop me every now and again and say to me: "We are in Heaven because you challenged young people to go. You raised missionary money. You came to our country with the Gospel. Now we want to thank you for your part in our salvation." That, my friend, will be my greatest joy in Heaven.

Will it be yours? Will anyone ever express his or her appreciation to you for what you did? Will there be anyone from the heathen world who will recognize you? Not if you have done all your Christian work in your own country. Not unless you have invested something in the regions beyond.

Give according to your income lest God make your income according to your giving.

CHAPTER VIII

HOW CAN WE EVANGELIZE THE WORLD
IN THIS GENERATION?

IF I were to choose a text I would turn to Mark 13:10—
"The Gospel—The Gospel must—The Gospel must first—
The Gospel must first be published—The Gospel must first
be published among all nations."

I wish I could spend at least half-an-hour on every one of
these statements, for each one is of paramount importance,
but I only have time to deal with one. As a matter of fact I
am going to emphasize just one word, the word "published."
"The Gospel must first be *published* among all nations."

I believe it is God's plan that every man should have the
Gospel in his own tongue, and yet there are 2,000 languages
into which no portion of the Word of God has as yet been
translated. In English there have been more than 500 revi-
sions. Why should they be denied?

Do you realize that you owe everything you are to the
printed page? Had it not been for the Word of God you
would not have been a Christian. The Bible says, "Faith
cometh by hearing, and hearing by the Word of God." How
then can we expect the heathen to hear and be saved if they
do not even have it?

What was it that gave us the Reformation? You say it was
Martin Luther's preaching. I do not believe it was. Martin
Luther wrote nearly 100 books and circulated them through-
out Western Europe, and, as a result of the *writings* of Martin
Luther, there came the Reformation. Where would you have
been today if it had not been for the Reformation? The Dark
Ages would still be upon us and you in all probability would
be a Roman Catholic.

I believe that the greatest miracle of our day and generation is the increasing literacy around the world. Have you any idea as to how many people learn to read every week? Let me tell you. Three million people learn to read every seven days. What does that mean? It means that last week three million people who could not read one single word are able to read this week. It means that next week another three million people who cannot read a single word this week will be able to read next week. Three million people every week —one hundred and fifty million people a year.

That has never happened before in the 6,000 years of man's history on earth. Up until our generation only a handful of people have been able to read in comparison to the vast multitudes unable.

The Communists have the Answer

But what are they going to read? The Communists have the answer. They know something of the power of the printed page.

Do you know that the Communists printed two pieces of literature in a single year for every man, every woman, every boy, and every girl, on the face of the earth? What other nation has done that? No other nation has, but the Communists have.

Why, they even boast of having taken China by means of the printed page. For twenty-five years before the Russian Revolution the Communists poured their literature into Russia.

Some time ago the United Nations gave the number of different books printed by five of the leading nations of the world. Which nation do you think came first? Russia came first with 60,000 different titles. Which nation came second? The most literate nation on the face of the earth—Japan— with 24,000 titles. Great Britain came third with 19,000 and India fourth with 18,000. Which nation do you think came last of all? The United States of America. During that year America only printed 12,000 different titles. Now, tell me, which nation believes in the power of the printed page? The United States with 12,000 or Russia with 60,000?

Do you know that during one year Russia printed no less than one billion books and translated 5,000? During the same year the United States only translated 800 and Great Britain 600. Again I ask, Which nation believes in the power of the printed page?

Gandhi's grandson—Gandhi of India—said the other day in Los Angeles, "The missionaries taught us to read, but the Communists gave us the books." Think of it, if you will. "The missionaries taught us to read, but the Communists gave us the books." Why didn't the missionaries give them the books? Because the churches that had sent out the missionaries had never caught the vision. They had failed to place the ammunition in the hands of their missionaries. So, after having taught the people to read, they allowed the Communists to come along and supply the reading material.

JEHOVAH'S WITNESSES ARE ON THE JOB

Yes, and let me tell you something else, believe it or not, the False Cults are on the job.

Do you realize that Jehovah's Witnesses have the largest religious printing press in the world? Why is it that the Christian Church does not have the largest press? Simply because the Christian Church has never realized the value of literature. Do you know how many magazines that one press prints every minute? Every sixty seconds that one press produces 500 magazines (eighty-four million in a single year). Where are these magazines circulated? Through the English speaking world? Yes. But mainly in the Orient, Asia, Africa and South America.

Are Jehovah's Witnesses getting results? Does it pay to get out the printed page? Jehovah's Witnesses held a Baptismal Service in New York some time ago, where, at that one service they baptized 7,136 converts. How many has your church baptized? How many have all the churches of America baptized? How many were baptized on the Day of Pentecost? Less than half that number. And this is the point, every convert was won by the means of the printed page. Does it pay? Jehovah's Witnesses think it does.

Did you ever see the little inexpensive Kingdom Halls that Jehovah's Witnesses have? You have never known them to build a cathedral. Why? Because they realize that the message is more important than the building. Therefore, they put their money into the message, not into the building.

That is where the Christian Church has made its greatest mistake. We have been putting our money into buildings instead of the message. It is the message that is dynamite. "The Gospel is the power of God unto salvation." Not the building but the message.

In one year, according to the National Council of Churches, there were built in the United States of America, 6,000 new churches at a cost of one billion dollars. When I read that, I said to myself, "I wish I could somehow stop that building programme for just twelve months and get my hands on that billion dollars. If I could put that billion dollars into the message, this world, I believe, could be evangelized within a matter of years." Now I am not against building new churches. I think we ought to build adequately for our needs. But I am against building luxurious cathedrals when the world is so desperately in need of the message of God's salvation.

Do you know what one billion dollars would do? It would put a New Testament in every home on the face of the earth.

How many church buildings were there when the Apostle Paul commenced his great missionary work? Not one. Yet we think we must have Home Bases before we can do anything. Paul went out before even a single church building had been erected.

My friends, we will have to decide whether we are going to put our money into the building or into the message if we are ever going to evangelize the world.

During a single year the Seventh Day Adventists invested $21,000,000 in the printed page in 218 languages. They, too, believe in the power of the message.

World Literature Crusade

That is why I became interested in World Literature Crusade. They are out to place the Gospel message in every home in a given country, thus reaching every family and, ultimately, every creature with the Gospel. They do it in a systematic way so that no one will be overlooked.

The messages are not printed in America because they would then be foreign and, on account of the rising tide of nationalism, nothing foreign is acceptable.

They are printed in foreign countries—the country of distribution—because the work can be done so much cheaper, less than one-fifth the cost in America.

If the messages were printed in America, there would be transportation and duty charges and these they want to avoid.

How much do the missionaries pay for them? Absolutely nothing at all. They get the literature free-of-charge. All they have to do is to agree not to miss a single home in their territory.

The messages are not printed in thousands, they are printed in millions. It is a world task and it requires a world vision.

The work has been almost finished in Japan. Ninety per cent of the homes where 94 million people live have had a Gospel message. What has been the result? No less than 329,000 Japanese have written in asking to be enrolled in a Bible Correspondence Course, requesting more literature, or inquiring about the way of salvation, according to Rev. Ken McVety, who lives in Japan and directs the work.

Most homes in South Korea, so far as we know, have had a Gospel message. What has been the result there? No less than 400,000 Koreans have written in indicating their interest in the Gospel, requesting additional literature, and asking to be enrolled in a Bible Correspondence Course.

How could you get results like that in any other way? All the missionaries in a given country could not produce such results. The printed page is God's method for our day and generation.

Jesus said "every creature." The only way you can reach every creature is to reach every home and family. That is why I endorse Wycliffe Bible Translators. They are obeying the command to give every tribe the Word of God. There is no other way that I know of to carry out our Lord's orders.

In some areas it only costs 14c to win a soul to Jesus Christ by means of the printed page. That means that there is no cheaper way to carry on missionary work. If we can systematically put a copy of the printed page in every home in a country we will have reached "every creature" in that country, for we will have reached every member of the family. Our missionaries can organize a group of workers and send them from door to door, from house to house, with the message. That was Paul's method and therefore it is scriptural. He evangelized from "house to house," so as to reach "every creature" with the Gospel message. We cannot do better than to follow his example.

BEHIND THE IRON CURTAIN

My books are now in 100 different languages and we are putting them into more all the time. My Gospel messages are going out in hundreds of thousands. I believe the work of tract distribution should be followed up with a booklet containing a Gospel message.

Recently I had three books published in the Polish language in Warsaw, Poland, behind the Iron Curtain. That was a miracle. These are now being distributed all over Poland by the 280 churches that are still open. I do not write off a country simply because it goes behind the Iron Curtain, the

Bamboo or the Purple Curtain. If I cannot send in missionaries, I may be able to send in the Gospel. It is the Gospel that is the power of God unto salvation.

Some time ago a certain Bible School sent its students out to a very busy street to give out Gospel tracts on the sidewalk. Do you know what happened? Within ten minutes' time the whole of the street was simply littered with torn Gospel tracts. The people had taken them, had glanced at them, had seen that they were tracts, and then had torn them to pieces and thrown them away. That is how much the printed page is appreciated in America.

I have travelled all over foreign countries. I have given out Gospel tracts everywhere. I have seen thousands upon thousands of tracts distributed. Do you know, I have never yet seen a native tear up a Gospel tract, or a Salvation booklet? When you hand a native in a foreign land a tract or a booklet, he will thank you for it most graciously, and then sit down right where he is—in the train or the bus or the street car—and read it unashamed. Literature is appreciated in foreign lands. That is why I am putting my money into "foreign literature" rather than into literature for this country.

On one of our Russian fields the Chairman called all the pastors and missionaries to the front, and taking one of my books in the Russian language, he tore it to pieces, after which he handed each missionary and pastor, just one page. That page was folded very carefully and put in an inside pocket and then taken back into the far interior. There the missionary gathered the villagers around him and read it word for word; knowing nothing of what went before or what came after. It was read until many had memorized it. Where there is a famine of the Word it is treasured as gold.

Let anyone take an automobile, load it with tracts and drive through France or Italy, or any other country, and just give out Gospel tracts, and he will have a ministry that will count for Eternity, even if he is unable to preach in the language of the people. God uses the printed page.

"Give Us the Tools"

It was during the time of the last World War. France had fallen. The United States had not yet come in. Great Britain was standing alone with her back against the wall expecting almost instant invasion. Sir Winston Churchill, the Prime Minister, decided to speak directly to the American people. I was driving along the highway with my wife. I drew my car to the side and turned off the engine so that I would not miss a word, and then I tuned in London, England.

The Prime Minister only spoke for two or three minutes, but he said something that I have never forgotten from that day to this. Sir Winston Churchill, in speaking to the American people, said this: "Give us the tools and we will finish the job." From that day to this I have been going up and down the land, speaking to congregations of all denominations on behalf of our 44,000 Protestant missionaries, and I have been saying, "Give us the tools and we will finish the job."

That is what I say to you now. As fast as the money comes in the message goes out. We have the workers. We have the organization. All we need are the funds with which to do the work. Have you ever invested in the printed page? Have you ever given anything to get the message out? May God help you to do what you can. "Give us the tools and we will finish the job."

CHAPTER IX

THE PAULINE METHODS

THE Student Volunteer Movement adopted as its slogan: "The Evangelization of the World in This Generation." Well do I recall in my student days the enthusiasm of John R. Mott, Sherwood Eddy, Robert E. Speer and others. That was fifty years ago, and still the world is unevangelized. Why the failure? Did the Student Volunteer Movement attempt an impossible task? Not if the Pauline plan for world evangelism had been adopted and carried out.

For over a hundred years now we have been sending out missionaries to be pastors of native churches, and thus God's order has been reversed. Our methods as a Church have not been scriptural. Hence, the world is still unevangelized in spite of all our efforts.

Paul, the greatest and most successful missionary the world has ever known, did not become a pastor. He travelled, preached, won converts, organized churches, placed them under native leadership, and passed on. He did not attempt to change the manners and customs of the people. The Gospel, where necessary, did that. He placed responsibility upon the natives themselves, made the churches founded self-supporting and self-propagating, and that from the very first. He founded no colleges, built no hospitals and erected no church buildings. The natives provided for their own needs.

MISSIONARY METHODS

During my world tours I made a very careful study of missionary methods. In many fields I found foreign missionaries acting as pastors of native churches, a thing unknown in Scripture. In one country, for instance, I visited a number of leaders who had been sent out as missionaries, in some cases, twenty, twenty-five and even thirty years ago. These men had settled down in various towns and cities, and, after preaching for some time, had won a number of converts, whom they had organized into a church. And during all these years they had remained themselves in charge as pastors. Consequently their influence had not been felt beyond the confines of their local work.

I do not mean to insinuate that these missionaries have not done good work. Certainly they have been a blessing to the locality in which their church has been situated. But after twenty, twenty-five and thirty years of service they have to admit that the country in which they have laboured for so long, and in some cases even the city in which they live and preach, is still unevangelized. What a tragedy! They became pastors of native churches instead of Pauline evangelists.

What, then, should they have done? They should have followed the example of Paul. They should have kept the evangelization of the entire country constantly in mind, adopting the scriptural methods that would have made this possible. The business, the one and only business of the foreign missionary, is to train native workers, and put responsibility upon them. They should be appointed as evangelists or teachers according to their gifts and sent forth to evangelize their country. They should be ordained as pastors and elders and placed in charge of churches. Each church should be self-governing, and like a hive it should repeatedly swarm. Thus new churches would be constantly springing up and in a short time the entire country would be evangelized.

In one country I visited I found a number of foreign missionaries who had become pastors, who were unwilling to allow their young men, gifted though they were, to go from the mother church in order to evangelize other sections of the country.

The Missionary Societies that see Paul's vision are endeavouring to adhere strictly to scriptural methods. They are keeping evangelism to the forefront. They are not specializing in hospitals, for they realize that institutional work is the responsibility of the State. There are many hospitals in the foreign field in which no spiritual work is allowed. They are not building colleges for they do not believe in educating the unsaved. Moreover, they have learned from experience that education in the hands of an enemy of the Cross is a most dangerous weapon. In fact, most of the trouble in China and India, as well as other countries, comes from the student class. Nor do they establish Theological Seminaries. To put a native through a long course of study is to rob him of his vision, turn him into a student and send him forth with a superiority complex. All that a man needs to begin with is a knowledge of the fundamental truths of the Gospel and how to give them out. If a country is to be evangelized it must have evangelists. The one and only thing to do is to preach the Gospel. "Go ye into all the world, and preach the Gospel to every creature," commanded Jesus. Preach it everywhere, in the bazaars and market places, on the street corners, in halls and homes, anywhere, everywhere, but *preach, preach, preach,* and preach the *Gospel,* for the Gospel is the power of God unto salvation.

NATIVE BIBLE SCHOOLS

Hence, in one country there was established a sort of Home Bible School, where an evangelistic course of intensive Bible study lasting only three months was given. So short was the term that none of those taking the course had time to become students. They remained evangelists. And at the end of the three months the fire was burning brighter than at the beginning. As evangelists they were then sent forth to preach the Gospel over a widely scattered area. After they evangelized for a year, they were brought back for another three or four months of intensive training. Then sent out again.

Most foreign missionaries seem afraid to trust the native worker. I remember one such. His furlough was long overdue, but he hesitated to leave. For years past he had taken full charge of the station and was alone responsible for everything. Not a single native worker had he trained. At last the hour arrived when he was simply compelled to go.

It so happened that a visiting missionary was spending a few days with him, one who knew and practiced the scriptural method. Seeking to solve the problem the visitor requested his much worried friend to call the leading natives of the congregation before him, with a view to finding out which of them, if any, could be entrusted with responsibility.

Then, to his amazement, his visiting friend took this untrained and doubtful material and appointed each one to a position of trust. One was to be the pastor, another the treasurer, a third the superintendent of the entire work. Others, evangelists, elders, etc. Thus each one, to his own surprise, was given a responsible position. The tired, overworked missionary took his furlough. A year passed by. At last he returned expecting to find disaster. To his amazement he found that every man had made good. The work had prospered as never before. Scores of souls had been won to Christ. The church was in a flourishing condition. For miles around the country had been evangelized. Money had been contributed, repairs made to the church, and other chapels erected.

The natives for the first time in their lives had been made conscious of their responsibility. In fear and trembling, unused to being trusted, they had gone about their work, but it was the scriptural method and God blessed. What a revelation to the missionary who thought he had to do it all and hence could not be spared!

The reason so many missionaries are content to settle down as pastors is because they only see their own local work; whereas their vision should take in, not merely the village or town in which they labour, but the whole country. Their task is not only the evangelization of their own community, but a nation.

ORDAIN ELDERS

But now for God's plan for the establishment of local churches. How is it to be done? That is to say, how is it to be done without foreign funds? What is the scriptural method?

Paul, you remember, evangelized, won converts, formed them into little churches, and appointed elders. Herein lies the secret. He took two or three men and placed them as elders over the flock. Now these men did not give up their daily occupations. But they became the overseers of the church. They called the church together for worship at regular intervals. They presided at the Lord's Table. They baptized the new converts. They read the Scriptures and led in prayer. They visited the sick.

Here, for instance, are a number of cities, towns, and villages. Our native evangelists, Paul's company, trained in our Bible School, commence a campaign of evangelization. The Word is preached, tracts distributed, and personal work done, and finally, a number of converts are won. But they are scattered over a wide area, and so they are formed into little groups, churches. From each group the most gifted of the men are selected and ordained as elders. Two will suffice. Three would be better. These elders are placed over their own groups. Thus the church meets regularly under their leadership. They may not be able to preach, but one of them can read the Word. Another may be gifted to expound it. And all can pray.

These churches will, of course, grow. That is, if they are normal, living organisms. When they become too large, they will just naturally swarm. Another little church will be born. The elders already appointed have power to appoint others, and to organize other churches. Thus they will multiply rapidly until, in a short time, there will be little churches scattered all over the country.

Now a church may become strong enough in certain centres to require the whole time of a pastor. The pastor may be one of the elders, who, if necessary, can be trained in the Bible

School. Or he may be one of the evangelists already trained.
He is now supported by the native church. He is not sent to a
weak church and supported by foreign money, but he is called
to a strong church and supported by the natives themselves.

In some districts converts have had no Communion for two
or three years, simply because there was no foreign pastor and
the bishop was not able to get around. For they had been
taught that only properly ordained pastors had authority to
baptize and preside at the Lord's Table. Whereas, from
among themselves, elders should have been ordained, who
could have done everything required.

Never can we send out enough foreign missionaries to evangelize the world. Never can we support enough native pastors
to place one in every town and village world-wide. But we can
found a Bible School. We can send out a Dean. We can train
native pastors and evangelists. The evangelists can go everywhere, as Paul did, evangelizing. They can form the converts
into local churches even if there are only two or three at first.
"For where two or three are gathered together in My Name,
there am I in the midst of them," said Jesus. And that constitutes a New Testament Church. They can appoint or ordain
elders from among the converts that the life of the church
may be maintained and developed. These churches can
multiply and organize others. And thus whole countries can
be evangelized.

The Native is the Key

But let us turn, in closing, to Acts 14:23. Paul and his
company of evangelists had travelled from city to city,
according to God's plan, and many converts had been won
and churches established. They did not remain permanently
anywhere, nor was there any thought of settling down as
pastors. Later on they made a second tour, and later again a
third. Thus they encouraged the churches. "And when they
had *ordained them elders in every church*, and had prayed
with fasting, they commended them to the Lord, on whom
they believed." And then—they left them.

The fact is, we have built "up" instead of "out." Such has ever been the policy of Roman Catholicism, and Protestantism has made the same mistake. In organization we have gone from laity and priest to pope, and in buildings, from homes and halls to cathedrals. God told us to build *out*, to evangelize, but, ignoring His plan, we have built *up*. And so today we are over-burdened with property and top-heavy with machinery and organization.

Whereas had we followed the Pauline method, we would have found the burden light. It solves the financial problem. Large gifts for educational and medical buildings are unnecessary. Native evangelists are accustomed to native food and ways of living, and thereby the heavy expense of setting up a foreign establishment is saved, including furniture, imported foods and clothing, etc. Allowances are much less, as the evangelists are able to live comfortably in their accustomed way. The heavy expense of bringing foreign workers home every few years for furlough is saved.

A foreign language, with foreign customs and ways of thinking, does not have to be learned, so that much valuable time is saved. A foreign worker seldom ever learns perfectly the idioms of a native language and so always has a handicap. Our evangelists have this advantage from the first. They are at home with native manners and customs, and so do not cause offence.

My brethren, you may or may not agree with all that I have said. But one thing you cannot deny. Thus far we have failed to evangelize the world. Then we must admit that something is wrong. Have we ever thought that it might be our methods? Will the plan generally in vogue work? I think we must all agree that it will not. Then why not consider another? A plan tried and tested by the Early Church. A plan fitted to every country the world over. A plan that succeeds wherever it is put into practice. A plan that completely solves the financial problem. A plan through which the Holy Spirit can operate. God's plan. God's way.

CHAPTER X

CHRIST'S THREEFOLD COMMISSION

IN CHRIST'S Threefold Commission we have God's complete programme for the missionary enterprise in this dispensation. This threefold Commission is expressed in three simple words—look, pray and go.

LOOK

"Say ye not, There are yet four months and then cometh harvest? Behold, I say unto you, Lift up your eyes, and look on the fields; for they are white already to harvest" (John 4:35).

Thousands have no vision or knowledge of the need; hence great sums are wasted on expensive church buildings and equipment, while millions perish without even a mud hut in which to hear the Good News. One real look through the eyes of Jesus Christ and we will sink our funds not in bricks and mortar, luxurious Bible Training Schools and expensive institutions, but in the souls of men.

Oh, then, let us look; look as we have never looked before. And as we see in vision the teeming millions of China and India with the benighted multitudes of Africa and South America, let us listen again to the Master's words and catch a glimpse of the urgency of the need. "Behold, I say unto you, Lift up your eyes, and look on the fields; for they are white already to harvest."

Have you ever seen a harvest in our great Canadian Northwest? Then you know what it means. How urgent! How important that labourers be rushed off in train-loads. And why? Simply because the harvest must be gathered at once or it will be lost, and lost forever.

So it is with the whitened fields of souls. This generation can only reach this generation. Therefore, "What thou doest do quickly." If labourers do not hurry off at once, if we fail to do our utmost, this harvest, this generation will be lost forever. This may be our last opportunity to show our Lord how much we love Him. Some of us may soon be gone, for "the night cometh when no man can work." For many "the day is far spent." There are those who up to the present have lived for self and self alone. And now their years are numbered. Never yet have they manifested their love to Jesus Christ in any worth while way. Oh, then, let us be up and doing. Our last opportunity will soon be gone. In God's name, let us lift up our eyes and look, look on the fields white already to harvest!

PRAY

Humanly speaking the task is absolutely impossible. There are more heathen today than there were a century ago in spite of what we have done. What is the solution? "Money," replies one. "Let us gather together millions of dollars and we can evangelize the world." "Men," answers another. "Give us sufficient men to go and we will accomplish the task in this generation." No, friend, that is not God's method. Neither money nor men will do it.

Listen: "The harvest truly is plenteous, but the labourers are few." There you have the difficulties of the task, a great harvest and an inadequate number of harvesters. But hark! The Master continues to speak. Thank God, He has the solution and the problem is solved. "Pray ye therefore the Lord of the harvest, that He will send forth labourers into His harvest" (Matt. 9:37-38).

We have by far too many labourers now, labourers, I mean, of the wrong kind. They do not know their business, nor how to garner in the ripened harvest. With their Modern Theology and Social-uplift ideas they have sought to do what can never be done. Would to God they could be sent home!

What a blessing it would be to countless thousands! Our business is to "pray the Lord of the harvest, that He will send forth labourers." And when God sends men He always sends the right kind. This then is the secret—PRAY.

Go

1. *To the Nations.*
   "Go ye therefore and teach all nations" (Matt. 28:19).

The Bridegroom must have some from every tongue and tribe. "A great multitude, which no man could number, of all nations, and kindreds, and people, and tongues, stood before the throne" (Rev. 7:9). This is borne out in Acts 15:14, "God did visit the Gentiles to take out of them a people for His name." Hence, we have in Mark 13:10 these prophetic words: "And the Gospel must first be published among all nations," with the promise in Matthew, "and then shall the end come." Therefore, "Why speak ye not a word of bringing back the king?" This Paul declared to be his aim, namely, "To preach the Gospel in the regions beyond" (2 Cor. 10:16). Such, too was the plan of Jesus Himself. "All men seek for Thee," they told Him. "Let us go into the next towns that I may preach there also" (Mark 1:35-39) was His answer. And in Luke 4:43 He is even more emphatic. "I must preach the kingdom of God to other cities also: for therefore am I sent," He insisted. Then in Acts 1:8 we are definitely commissioned to a world-wide testimony, even "unto the uttermost part of the earth."

This, then is to be our vision. Not the duplicating of existing missionary agencies; rather we are to work in places still untouched. "Unoccupied areas," "where Christ has not been named," "the regions beyond," "farther, still farther into the night," "the neglected fields." These are our watchwords, this our glorious mission.

2. *To the Individual.*

"Go ye into all the world, and preach the Gospel to every creature" (Mark 16:15).

This is our responsibility and obligation to the individual. "When I say unto the wicked, thou shalt surely die; and thou givest him not warning, nor speakest to warn the wicked from his wicked way, to save his life; the same wicked man shall die in his iniquity; but his blood will I require at thine hand" (Ezek. 3:18).

What about the guilt of the man who finds a broken rail, but neglects to flag the train; or the one who watches a blind man about to fall over a precipice and neglects to call; or the one who sees another drowning and neglects to reach out a hand; or the one who notices a house on fire and neglects to give the alarm?

We have now been brought face to face with our individual responsibility. And again the awful question, "Am I my brother's keeper?" demands an answer. "Every creature." These are the Master's words. We will have to get back to the anointed vision of Dr. A. B. Simpson, when he wrote:

> "A hundred thousand souls a day,
> Are passing one by one away,
> In Christless guilt and gloom;
> Without one ray of hope or light,
> With future dark as endless night,
> They're passing to their doom."

Oh, child of God, what are you doing? What have you done? How will you face them? Can you bear the thought? Your Master's Commission, clear, plain and emphatic, the appalling need brought before you again and again, and yet you never raised a hand. The plate was passed and almost indifferently you tossed on a ten-dollar bill, and that was the measure of your interest for a whole year. With that your duty to missions ended. And you spend more in one week on yourself. God have mercy on you!

"O Church of Christ, what wilt thou say
When in the awful judgment day,
They charge thee with their doom?"

How much treasure have you laid up in Heaven? Where are your riches? In some earthly bank, where you must part with them sooner or later? Or have you consumed all on yourself? If such is the case you will enter Heaven a poor man. Think of it! A pauper in Heaven. No one to meet you because no investment in souls. God help us to store up treasure in Heaven by investing in precious souls here. "Lay not up for yourselves treasures upon earth, but lay up for yourselves treasures in heaven" (Matt. 6:19). This is the command of Jesus Christ. Are we prepared to obey?

Do you know that one hundred dollars a year for missions is less than two dollars per week? Think of it! What is your salary? Fifteen, twenty-five, forty dollars a week? Then that means thirteen, twenty-three or thirty-eight dollars each week on yourself, and only the paltry sum of two dollars for the evangelization of the world. What a crime! What an unequal division!

Beloved, I am done! My message has been given. The responsibility now rests upon you. What are you going to do about it? What is your part? Christ's Threefold Commission has now been set before you. Look! Pray. Go! You can look and you can pray. And if you cannot go, you can make it possible for those to go whom God in answer to prayer would thrust forth into the whitened harvest fields. Will you do it?

CHAPTER XI

THE MISSIONARY CALL

WHAT constitutes a call? Is there any way of knowing the will of God? How can one be sure? I think there is. In fact, I am certain. God would not leave His servants in darkness.

But let me give you James Gilmour's experience. It is well worth quoting. How was he called, and why did he go to the Mongols? This is how he puts it:

"Is the kingdom a harvest field? Then I thought it reasonable that I should seek to work where the work was most abundant and the workers fewest. Labourers say they are overtaxed at home; what, then, must be the case abroad, where there are wide-stretching plains already white to harvest with scarcely here and there a solitary reaper?

"To me the soul of an Indian seemed as precious as the soul of an Englishman, and the Gospel as much for the Chinese as for the European; and as the band of missionaries was few compared with the company of ministers at home, it seemed to me clearly to be my duty to go abroad.

"But I go out as a missionary, not that I may follow the dictates of common sense, but that I may obey that command of Christ, 'Go into all the world and preach.' This command seems to be strictly a missionary injunction; so that, apart altogether from choice and other lower reasons, my going forth is a matter of obedience to a plain command: and in place of seeking to assign a reason for going abroad, I would prefer to say that I have failed to discover any reason why I should stay at home."

Gilmour went in response to the Great Commission. His Captain ordered him to "go" and he went. He went because he could find no adequate reason for staying at home. He went to the foreign field because, as he says, there the workers were fewest. What a heroic decision!

What was Charles T. Studd's reason for going? Studd, you remember, gave away a fortune—$145,000. He could have lived at home in great luxury, but he chose rather to give away all that he had and go to China as a missionary. Why? Strange as it may seem, it was the statement of an atheist that started him on his way. It so gripped him when he read it that he felt he must leave all and follow Jesus Christ. Here it is:

"Did I firmly believe, as millions say they do, that the knowledge and practice of religion in this life influences destiny in another, religion would mean to me everything. I would cast away earthly enjoyment as dross, earthly cares as follies, and earthly thoughts and feelings as vanity. Religion would be my first waking thought, and my last image before sleep sank me into unconsciousness. I would labour in its cause alone. I would take thought for the morrow of eternity only. I would esteem one soul gained for Heaven worth a life of suffering. Earthly consequences should never stay my hand, nor seal my lips. Earth, its joys and griefs, would occupy no moment in my thoughts. I would strive to look upon eternity alone, and on the immortal souls around me, soon to be everlastingly happy or everlastingly miserable. I would go forth to the world and preach to it in season and out of season, and my text would be, 'What shall it profit a man, if he shall gain the whole world, and lose his own soul?' "

Is that the way you feel? Have you, too, felt the urge? Does the Word of God burn like a fire in your heart? Have you no rest day or night because you do not go?

"When I say unto the wicked, O wicked man, thou shalt surely die; if thou dost not speak to warn the wicked from his way, that wicked man shall die in iniquity; but his blood will I require at thine hand. Nevertheless, if thou warn the wicked of his way to turn from it; if he do not turn from his way, he shall die in his iniquity; but thou has delivered thy soul" (Ezek. 33:8-9).

THE NEED AND THE URGE

That means, of course, that the need is the call. Men are dying. You have the message of life. Are you going to withhold it from them? The responsibility rests upon you.

And yet the need of itself is not sufficient. There must be the ability to meet that need. Do you feel that you have the necessary qualifications? For instance, there is a language to be learned. Can you learn it? Are you young enough, or is it already too late? There is your health to be considered. Have you the physique able to endure a tropical climate? Then, too, a fair amount of education is imperative, education both secular and theological. Do you qualify?

Providential circumstances will prove a real factor in guidance. Doors will miraculously open, and your need will be supplied. Funds either earned or given for your training, will be forthcoming. Obstacles and hindrances will be overcome or taken away. And at last the Board of God's choice will accept you. Then you will get your outfit and your passage money, and, if necessary, the promise of your first year's support.

To me the call is that divine urge, that compelling impulse, that passion within that makes it impossible for me to resist. There is something within that is calling, ever calling. I am restless. I am like a hunter's dog on the leash, straining to get away. It is that irresistible "must."

The divine fire burns within my heart. I rise from my desk and rapidly pace the floor, praying, crying to God. My mind is not on what I am doing. I see the distant fields. I feel that, come what may, I have no choice but to go. I am not satisfied to settle down where I am. One time I expressed it like this:

> *Hark! 'tis a Voice that calls to me*
> *Out of the depths of mystery.*

It was that inner Voice that spoke to my soul, and called me into the ministry and to the mission fields of the world. I can't explain it, except to speak of it as an "urge" that was with me night and day. That urge I followed, and I have never been disappointed.

> "Stir me, Oh! stir me, Lord—I care not how,
> But stir my heart in passion for the world;
> Stir me to give, to go, but most to pray,
> Stir, till the Blood-red banner be unfurled
> O'er lands that still in heathen darkness lie,
> O'er deserts where no Cross is lifted high."

If you really want to hear God's voice, and if you want to do His will, I can tell you how you may find out whether or not He has called you to the foreign field. Just do two things.

First, start praying about your life's work, and pray every day. Set aside a time to wait on God about it. Pray "Lord, what wouldst thou have me to do?" Every day talk to God about it.

Second, as you pray, read missionary biography. When I was a student I purchased a whole shelf of biographies, and read two or three chapters each day. You young women should be perfectly familiar with the life stories of Ann Judson, Mary Slessor, and other missionary heroines. You young men should know the lives of Livingstone, Moffat, MacKay, Gilmour, Morrison, Taylor and other great missionary heroes.

Why do I tell you to study biography? Because in this twentieth century you are living in an atmosphere in which God cannot speak to you. If you will read missionary biography you will be putting yourself into an atmosphere where God can talk to you.

Hence as you read biography, and then pray about your life's work day by day, you will hear the voice of God. Before long you will be burdened for some particular field, and after you have finished your training in Bible School or College, you will find yourself in the place of God's choosing for you.

That is the way most missionaries have heard God's call.

As I said before, it is the Divine urge. It is the voice of the Holy Spirit telling you to go, and if you disobey you will do so at your peril. You can never be happy except in the centre of God's will.

SATAN'S OPPOSITION

But no sooner will you decide to become a missionary than Satan will do everything in his power to discourage you. He may make it difficult for you to get the money you need to secure your training. He may turn the members of your own family against you. If he cannot succeed in any other way, he will do what he has done in hundreds of cases. He will get you young women interested in some young man who has no idea of ever becoming a missionary, and if you marry him you will never be a missionary. He will get you young men interested in some young woman who is not planning upon going to the foreign field, and if you marry her that will be the end of your missionary work forever.

I cannot tell you how many have come to in middle age, and have said, "Dr. Smith, God called me to be a missionary but I married a man who was not going, and now we have a family. We are in middle life and it is too late. I have missed God's best and now I must take His second best." And I have had them break down and weep. Listen, young people, if God has called you and you have become an active volunteer, then you have no right to even keep company with anyone except someone who is travelling in your direction, and if you do that you will both reach the same destination.

Thus you will be called, and thus you will be guided, and if you will faithfully follow these suggestions, God will lead you into the most glorious work ever committed to man. You will become a missionary, your life will be invested in a worthwhile work, and, conscious of the leading of the Lord, you will never be disappointed.

You can do what millions of others have done if you want to. You can settle down to the monotony of American life, get married, raise children, work, retire, die and be forgotten, or—you can become a pioneer, a trail-blazer, invest your life in a great adventure for God, and be the first to give some unreached tribe the Gospel, and be remembered forever. Which is it to be? It is for you to decide.

John G. Paton argued this way: "I clearly saw that all at home had free access to the Bible and the means of grace, with Gospel light shining all around them, while the poor heathen were perishing without even the chance of knowing all God's love and mercy to men."

Will you then listen to His voice and answer, "Here am I, Lord, send me?"

CHAPTER XII

THERE are two kinds of volunteers, passive and active. The passive volunteer says, "Lord, here am I." Next year he says it again, and five years later he is saying once more, "Lord, I am still here."

Here he is, here he was, and here he always will be. He has an idea that he has to wait until he hears a supernatural voice, or until God reaches down, picks him up and transplants him to some foreign land. God cannot use passive volunteers.

The active volunteer says, "Lord, here am I, send me." He puts a "go" into his volunteering, and, setting his face like flint, he prays through hindrances and overcomes obstacles. By faith he opens closed doors, prays in, or earns, the money he needs for his training, and gets his preparation. Finally, he finds himself ready for his life's work.

Then, he applies to a Mission Board, and, if he is turned down, he applies to another. At last he is accepted. Then he prays in his outfit and passage money, and finally, after overcoming every obstacle, he reaches the field. Nothing is allowed to stand in his way. God can use active volunteers.

Most of the so-called Faith Missions (to distinguish them from denominational Boards) require you to have completed your High School education and to have successfully graduated from an accredited Bible Institute. If you are young enough you should take your college work as well, majoring in Bible. If you decide to go to a seminary be sure it is not one that will rob you of your missionary fervour. Make certain that it is pre-millennial and that it emphasizes evangelism.

To get too much training is impossible, provided you do

not lose your vision. But much depends upon your age. You should plan to leave for the field by the time you are twenty-five, if at all possible—in any case not later than twenty-eight. Hence, if you are near the age limit, get your Bible Training and be off, even if you are not a High School graduate.

All through your training you should be actively associated with some missionary church, for the day will come when you will need the recommendation of a pastor who knows you well, and the backing of a spiritual church. Boards depend to a large extent upon what the pastor has to say. See Acts 13:1-2; 15:3.

In addition to education you need some practical experience, for if God cannot use you at home, neither can He use you on the foreign field. Some kind of Christian service is absolutely essential. Do personal work, preach, take meetings, help in Rescue Missions, visit the sick. Learn to sacrifice, rough it, live by faith. Get all the practical experience you can. In other words, be a soul-winner at home before you go to a foreign field. There is nothing in the crossing of the ocean that will make you a missionary. Unless you are successful before you leave, you will not be after.

If you can secure an elementary knowledge of book-keeping and typewriting, it will be invaluable. Many missionaries lack business training, and it is important that accounts should be accurately kept.

If you are young enough and you have everything else you need, you should take a year in Medicine. Such a course is considered necessary by most Missions working in tropical regions. You will then know how to take care of yourself when you are sick, and other missionaries and Christians as well, besides relieving minor ailments among the natives, and thus making an opening for the Gospel.

Language study is always a problem. If, therefore, you can take an intensive course in Phonetics and Phonemics or a Linguistic course, you will find it a real timesaver.

When you are ready, apply to one of the Mission Boards carrying on work in the country to which you believe God has called you. If you write to them they will be glad to send you their literature, and, when you have completed your training, application forms. I would suggest that you keep in touch with the Mission under which you expect to serve, from the beginning. Study their literature, and learn as much as you can about the work.

In going to the field you should go under a Board that is prepared to accept financial responsibility. I believe in faith, but faith on behalf of the Board as well as the worker. The missionary has enough to contend with. It is up to the Board that sends to see that the money comes in so that full allowances can be paid and all emergency needs met.

Whatever you do, go under a well accredited Mission. Do not go under an inexperienced Board. You will find an approved Mission in almost every field.

There are still vast territories where the Gospel has never been preached. You may yet be a pioneer. If God has called you, do not hesitate to go. No greater honour can come to any man or woman than the honour of being a missionary. You will be the Lord's ambassador. Be faithful, and the Crown of Life will be yours. And when at last the Home Call comes, you will say with the sainted Brainerd, "I would not have spent my life otherwise for the whole world."

CHAPTER XIII

MISSIONARY HARDSHIPS

MISSIONARY work today is very different from what it was fifty years ago. And yet there are still pioneer fields where heroism is demanded and persecution rages. Trails there are that have never yet been blazed, where suffering is still the lot of those who venture.

"I want to remind the committee," said McKay of Uganda, "that within six months they will probably hear that one of us is dead. One of us at least—it may be I—will surely fall before that. But what I want to say is this: When the news comes, do not be cast down, but send someone else immediately to fill the vacant place."

That prediction was literally fulfilled. One by one the members of McKay's party either died of fever or were murdered by the natives, until, before long, he alone was left.

But why let hardships deter? Hear what David Brainerd had to say:

"Here I am, Lord, send me; send me to the ends of the earth; send me to the rough, the savage pagans of the wilderness; send me from all that is called comfort in earth, or earthly comfort: send me to death itself, if it be but in Thy service and to promote Thy kingdom."

Yes, and listen to Francis Xavier: "Yet more; Oh, my God, more toil, more agony, more suffering for Thee."

Here are C. T. Studd's words: "If Jesus Christ be God and died for me, then no sacrifice can be too great for me to make for Him."

Even death itself can be victorious. David Livingstone it was who exclaimed: "Death is a glorious event to one going to Jesus."

Strange it would be if one could read the life of William Carey of India and keep back the tears. Even the Directors of the East India Company opposed his work. Following is the idiotic resolution that they presented to Parliament, a resolution written in the blindness of prejudice and unbelief.

"The sending out of missionaries into our Eastern possessions is the maddest, most extravagant, most costly, most indefensible project which has ever been suggested by a moonstruck fanatic. Such a scheme is pernicious, imprudent, useless, harmful, dangerous, profitless, fantastic. It strikes against all reason and sound policy, it brings the peace and safety of our possessions into peril."

It may be of interest to point out that in 1796 the General Assembly of the Church of Scotland passed the following infamous resolution: "To spread the knowledge of the Gospel amongst barbarous and heathen nations, seems to be highly preposterous."

One speaker in the House of Commons said that he would rather see a band of devils let loose in India than a band of missionaries. Such was the opposition to missions when Carey set forth.

And yet, in the midst of his deepest trials, his heart nigh to breaking, he was able to write as follows: "Why is my soul disquieted within me? Things may turn out better than I expect. Everything is known to God, and God cares." What courage!

In Carey's day, the theologians believed that the command, "Go ye into all the world and preach the Gospel to every creature," was addressed to the apostles only, and had nothing to do with them at all. No wonder mission work was hard.

Finally, when he did go, he was burdened with two unsympathetic women, his wife and her sister, four helpless children, and a colleague who was an eccentric, and hopelessly in debt. In addition, he was completely misunderstood by the Society that sent him out, slandered by his enemies, and persecuted by the natives whom he had come to win.

Did ever man face the task of world-evangelism under more unfavourable circumstances? Yet he stood the test and became the father of modern missions. His life reads like a book of fiction.

Today, missionaries get home on furlough every few years. But not so the pioneers. Some of them never saw the homeland again for periods of fifteen or even twenty years; some only once or twice in a lifetime. Many of them went back never to return. Like David Livingstone and the martyred James Chalmers, they died at their post.

It would be hard to read the life of that lonely, bereaved figure, James Gilmour of Mongolia, and not realize something of the suffering through which he passed.

But of all those whose lives I have studied, no one has touched my heart like Judson of Burma. What Judson suffered, no tongue can tell. That awful nightmare in the Burmese prison will never be forgotten. Such anguish is beyond the power of human words to describe. How vividly Mrs. Morrow portrays it in her soul-stirring book, *The Splendour of God*.

DIFFICULTIES AND HARDSHIPS

No one would ever dream of living in the tropics unless he were either after money or souls. Only those who have done so know how the humid climate saps one's vitality and the unbearable heat makes life miserable. Think of the diseases of the tropics, the fevers, the insects and other pestilences. Who would exchange the invigorating frosts of the temperate zones for such a life?

Then, too, think of the difficulties of language study. It is no easy thing to master a new tongue. Many of God's servants have struggled with a foreign dialect until they have felt like giving up in despair.

Possibly the most difficult problem is that of finding congenial companions. Missionaries are human. Temperaments differ. So hot was the contention between Barnabas and Paul that they had to separate. Workers may be spiritual and yet so constituted that they cannot get on with each other.

Moreover, there is loneliness and separation to be considered, loneliness that every missionary must experience. The home he has known in childhood, scenes to which he has become accustomed, friends and relatives, modern streets and cities, civilization with all its comforts—these must be forsaken for an entirely different environment. He must live in a country where everything is strange. Periods of loneliness, never before experienced, will be his, loneliness that at times becomes almost unbearable.

And not only loneliness but sickness. And sickness where there are few, if any, hospitals, doctors or nurses. To be ill at home, surrounded by every comfort and with every variety of food, is one thing; but to be ill in a foreign land, in the midst of strangers, is another. The depression caused by fever —who can describe it? To follow David Livingstone through his numerous periods of sickness in the fever-infested jungles of Africa is to get some idea of what it means to be ill in a foreign land.

Perhaps the greatest hardship of all will be the leaving of the children behind, and that cross no one can understand except those who have borne it. For a few years the children remain on the field, but the time comes when they must leave and go to school, where, without father, without mother, they grow up, until, when their parents return on furlough, they scarcely recognize them. The heartbreak of life in a foreign land, with the children at home, thousands of miles away, is simply indescribable. Yet such burdens must be borne, and such difficulties faced, if the Gospel is to be proclaimed in the regions beyond.

THE THREE FREDS

Somewhere in the great dread forests of Brazil lies all that is mortal of three brave pioneers for the kingdom of Christ. Their spirits have joined the Lord triumphant around the throne. The full story of their last days may never be known to us here. It is known only by that band of wild, savage Indians, the Kayapos, who, as far as we can gather, ambushed and massacred them.

I refer to the Three Freds who were clubbed to death in 1935. This was their last message: "Brethren, stand by us as one man. Should the result be that which we least want, pray and send others out to continue what the Lord has commenced." In a letter they wrote as follows: "Should the Lord will that we be taken, our prayer is that more men and money will be rushed over to follow up this advance."

In another letter, written on the trail, they said: "At any time, on this advance, we expect arrows down on us; then when we meet the Indians, the Lord will have to work in a wonderful way to save us from their clubs, with which they have killed many others." But the Lord did not see fit to save them. Their lot was to be martyrdom.

A verse from Fenton-Hall's poem, himself a martyr for Christ, perhaps best expresses it:

> "And grant that if I die for Thee,
> O Jesus Christ, my Master,
> Those who behold, may by my death
> Thy Christhood come to know;
> O Christ, my Lord! so dwell in me,
> That even by my dying,
> Those watching may be drawn to find
> Thy Blood's redeeming flow."

Richard Williams was dying from starvation, a martyr's death. Among his last words were these: "I have felt—come life, come death—God's will would be my choice. Should anything prevent my ever adding to this, let all my beloved ones at home rest assured that I was happy beyond expression, and would not have changed situations with any man living. Let them also be assured that my hopes were full and blooming with immortality; that Heaven, and love, and Christ, were in my heart; that the hope of glory, the hope laid up for me in Heaven, filled my whole heart with joy and gladness, and that to me to live is Christ, to die is gain: that I can say, 'I am in a strait betwixt two, to abide in the body, or to depart and be with Christ, which is far better.' " Truly, Richard Williams had caught the vision.

ALLAN GARDINER

With him died the sailor saint, Captain Allan Gardiner. Slowly he starved to death. "A little rice, two cakes of chocolate, six mice, and one pound of pork," was all there was left to sustain the lives of himself and his heroic companions.

And yet this was the way he faced it: "My prayer is, that the Lord my God may be glorified in me whatever it may be, by life or death, and that He will, should we fall, vouchsafe to raise up, and send forth other labourers into this harvest, that His Name may be magnified, and His kingdom enlarged, in the salvation of multitudes from among the inhabitants of this pagan land."

As he neared the end, Gardiner, in spite of his awful predicament, wrote as follows: "Blessed be my Heavenly Father for the many mercies I enjoy: a comfortable bed, no pain or even cravings of hunger, though excessively weak, scarcely able to turn in my bed, I am, by His abounding grace, kept in perfect peace, refreshed with a sense of my Saviour's love and an assurance that all is wisely and mercifully appointed."

Finally, on lonely, hostile Patagonia, the last survivor passed to his reward. And thus the scene is pictured by Jesse Page:

"All was still now on that shore, and, in sight of the sky and the sea, the unburied martyrs lay. No slow and painful footsteps on the shingle now, no reverent words of praise and trust whispered by the faint breath of dying men. God had sent His messenger to stay the suffering of the saints, and they rested in peace. 'So, He giveth His beloved sleep.' "

At last their bodies were found, and a service was held.

"Three volleys of musketry were fired over the grave, and slowly the mourners returned to the ship. And once more the tide rose and fell on that desolate shore, and the sea-birds mingled their cries with the sobbing of the wind. The dirge of many waters sounded by the grave, while the snow, falling noiselessly, covered with its mantle of white the place where the saints slept."

Yes, indeed, Allan Gardiner and his brave companions had caught the vision. Not a convert did they win. Alone they suffered, their wives, loved ones, and families far away. Help came too late. Yet they gladly gave their lives for the savage Indians of dark, benighted Patagonia.

But did they die in vain? Ah, no! The blood of the martyrs soon became the seed of the Church, and a glorious harvest followed. Someone had to pioneer, and Gardiner answered the call. Can we do less?

CHAPTER XIV

THE MISSIONARY PROGRAMME

WHEN I was eighteen years of age I found myself among the Indians of British Columbia, some 4,000 miles from home. Before long I was living alone on an Indian Reserve, teaching school through the week, and preaching on Sundays.

I had to find my own firewood, and since there was only one tree that would burn when it was green, I had to take an Indian boy and locate that tree near enough to the shore so that when it was cut it would fall into the ocean. I could then lop off the branches and tow it to the village, where I was able to cut it up into firewood.

I drew my bed up close to the stove and saw to it that the fire kept burning all night. If, at any time, it died down, I awoke and replenished it. The nights were bitterly cold and I suffered much.

Of course, I had to do my own cooking. I had only a table, three or four chairs, and a rough home-made bed for furniture. Hence, I was compelled to endure all the hardships of frontier life in an Indian village, on the borders of Alaska.

In the commonly accepted idea of the word, I was a missionary. But I was not a pioneer. I was manning a missionary station; I was holding a fort; I was serving where others had served before me. For all the Indians to whom I was ministering had already been evangelized. Hence, I was building on another man's foundation. I had not gone to those who had never heard.

DAVID LIVINGSTONE

David Livingstone had much the same experience, only he went on. He wrote home to the Society, pointing out how necessary it was to move men away from the mission stations and scatter them throughout the densely populated country to the north. The Board did not agree, but Livingstone went, nevertheless.

He saw that he must leave the trenches and go over the top. He knew that defensive warfare would never avail, but that there must be an offensive. He believed in pioneer work, and so, turning his face toward the darkness, he penetrated farther and still farther into the night. "Anywhere, provided it be forward," was his challenging motto. And leaving the already evangelized sections of the country, he plunged into the great unknown. His objective was to reach peoples and tribes that had never heard.

Robert Moffatt understood it, for in writing to David Livingstone he had this to say: "Do not sit down in lazy contentment. Do not choose an old station. Push on to the vast unoccupied district of the north. In that direction on a clear morning, I have seen the smoke of a thousand villages. There, no missionary has ever been. There, sir, is your field."

That, my friends, is the work of the true missionary, for only thus can we hasten the coming of the King. God is calling today for pioneers. Why, then, build on another's foundation? Go to those who have never heard. Blaze new trails. Be a pioneer.

"Since it is true," inquired an African chief of David Livingstone, "that all who die unforgiven are lost for ever, why did your nation not come to tell us of it before now? My ancestors are all gone, and none of them knew anything of what you tell me."

We must turn from the policy of replacement to that of pioneering. For decades the Church has concentrated on the same localities instead of pressing on into the darkness beyond. Trail blazers are still needed. Pioneers must answer the call.

"I am debtor." Paul knew it and admitted it—debtor to Africa; debtor to China and India; debtor to South America and the islands of the sea. "I am debtor," and so are you, each one of us. Paul gave us the Gospel but woe betide us if we keep it for ourselves. We must give it to those "for whom nothing has been prepared."

> *I am debtor, cried the great apostle,*
> *I am ready, ready now to go*
> *To the regions where the Saviour's message*
> *No one yet has had a chance to know.*

> *I am debtor and must take the Gospel*
> *To the heathen nations everywhere;*
> *Farther and still farther must I hasten*
> *Through the lands of darkness and despair.*

Dan Crawford knew it. He was but a lad of nineteen when he left for Africa, an only son. In the little company at the Glasgow station stood his mother. When a friend spoke a word of comfort, she replied, "He spared not His Son."

Twenty-two years passed before she saw him again. Yes, twenty-two years, while he toiled in Africa without a furlough. He had buried his son, and there, amid loneliness indescribable, fever-stricken again and again, time after time nigh unto death, he lived and toiled and suffered. I heard him when I was a student in Chicago and I will never, never forget him. At fifty-six he died. Dan Crawford had caught the vision.

David Brainerd heard the call. "I declare, now I am dying, I would not have spent my life otherwise for the whole world." These were his words. And again: "I cared not where or how I lived, or what hardships I went through, so that I could but gain souls to Christ."

"If thou forbear to deliver them that are drawn unto death, and those that are ready to be slain; if thou sayest, behold, we knew it not; doth not He that pondereth the heart consider it? And He that keepeth thy soul, doth He not know it? And shall not He render to every man according to his works?" (Prov. 24:11, 12).

Our duty is plain. We must evangelize the world. That is God's programme for His Church. May we be true to the vision.

CHAPTER XV

MISSIONARY PRINCIPLES

AFTER visiting seventy different countries in Europe, Asia and America; after surveying and carefully studying missionary methods in various fields; after taking part in missionary conferences and conventions for years past; after conferring with leaders of many missionary societies; after extensive reading, prayer and meditation, I have come to the following definite conclusions regarding missionary work:

(1) OUR WORK MUST BE EVANGELICAL

There must be no higher criticism, no modernism in our ranks. Every worker must stand four-square for the great fundamentals of the Faith. No missionary must be engaged who doubts the virgin birth, the deity of Christ, His vicarious death, salvation by faith, the need of regeneration, the inspiration of the Bible, the bodily resurrection of Christ, and His pre-millennial coming, etc. To support any other is nothing short of a tragedy. A house divided against itself cannot stand. We must see to it that our money is not used to help the enemies of the Gospel.

(2) OUR WORK MUST BE EVANGELISTIC

We are to evangelize the world. To Christianize the nations in this dispensation is impossible, since it is not God's plan. Our business is to co-operate with the Holy Spirit in the taking out of "a people for His name."

We are not to major on hospitals or give ourselves over to medical work. We are not to erect schools and colleges and spend our time educating the heathen. We are not to give ourselves, primarily, to the social, political and industrial betterment of those who have no interest in our Christ. Nor are we to introduce our western civilization in an effort to change the manners and customs of the people. We can relieve simple ailments as we go about our work, or in clinics, but only to get a hearing for the Gospel. And of course we will teach both Christians and seekers to read and write so that they may be able to study the Bible. Nor will we forget the children. But we will not put these things first.

Our work is to preach the Gospel and we must not be sidetracked. Institutional work puts the cart before the horse. The Gospel must go first. Raw savages can be saved. Ignorant heathen can be transformed into saints. The by-products will all follow in due time, as needed. Let us put our money into the souls of men, and our investment will stand forever.

(3) OUR MISSIONARIES OUGHT NOT TO BE PASTORS OF NATIVE CHURCHES

Think, if you will, of Chinese and Africans becoming our pastors. How long before we would rebel? But furthermore, how dare we localize our work! The vision of the whole field, the whole world must ever be kept in view. As soon as converts have been won and a church formed, elders should be appointed to act as overseers of the flock, and the missionary pass on, following the example of Paul, to the unevangelized fields.

(4) THE CHIEF WORK OF THE MISSIONARY MUST BE THE TRAINING OF NATIVE CHRISTIANS

Never can we send out a sufficient number of foreign workers to occupy every village, town and city throughout the world. But we can, with a few missionaries, train enough native workers to evangelize every nation. That was the policy of Jesus. He trained the twelve, then the seventy, and sent them forth. Let us follow His example. Let every one of our missionaries choose and train his twelve and his seventy. The best way is by establishing temporary training camps, or by bringing them to a centrally located Bible School for short but intensive terms of study.

(5) NATIVE PASTORS AND CHURCHES SHOULD NOT BE SUPPORTED BY FOREIGN FUNDS

The work should be self-supporting, self-governing and self-propagating, and that from the first. No one can be healthy and strong while leaning on another. And the habit once started is hard to break. Churches have become weak and indolent rather than aggressive and powerful as a result of foreign support. The vision of evangelism and its responsibility has been lost, and the outcome, in many cases, has been most disastrous.

On the other hand, we must recognize "Paul's Company," the group of native evangelists, trained in our Bible Schools, who need help in opening up new territory. So long as they are doing pioneer work in unoccupied areas, and continually moving about, they are entitled to support, at least until the churches founded are strong enough to shoulder the burden.

(6) WE SHOULD MAKE IT A RULE TO AIM FOR THE LARGEST CENTRES OF POPULATION

That was Paul's method. He seldom went to the village; he went to the city. He never sought the back street; he sought the well-known, centrally located synagogue. He struck for the market place where everybody congregated. Within a few days or hours at the most, he had everyone talking. He planted the Gospel first of all in Ephesus, Corinth, Philippi, and Rome, all great world centres. And from these large cities it was sounded out to all the region round about.

(7) WE MUST CONCENTRATE ON THE UNOCCUPIED AREAS

If we want to bring back the King, if we want to hasten His coming, we must take the Gospel to the last tribe, the last people, the last nation. We must go to "the regions beyond," to the places where Christ has "not been named." That, too, was always Paul's method. He did not enjoy building on another man's foundation. The place of greatest need is always God's place of greatest opportunity. Jesus never forgot the "other towns" and the "other sheep."

(8) In matters of Finance there should be Information, Prayer and Faith

Information results in inspiration. To withhold information regarding either the work or the needs, is to deny God's people the spiritual blessing that would otherwise be theirs. Moreover, untold thousands will never even hear of the existence of many splendid efforts, unless large conventions and conferences are held to make the work known. Not only do missionary organizations need our help; we need the inspiration and blessing that a knowledge of their work and needs provides. To ask a new candidate to secure hundreds of dollars for transportation, equipment and support, and then forbid him to make it known, is simply absurd. We are not all called to be a George Muller.

But then, besides telling the people, we must tell God. Prayer and missions go hand in hand. The greatest of all help in missionary work is that of intercession. We must advance on our knees. God has promised to answer prayer, and if He does not, if we are forced to send short allowances, we should check up at once. Unless our policy works, it is useless. If we are going to trust God, we must really trust Him. He is able to move in the hearts of His people in answer to the prayer of faith and cause them to act on the information given, and contribute to the work.

(9) We should never go into Debt

"Owe no man anything," is His Word. To disobey is to court disaster. We have no right to go forward until God supplies the funds. Let us get our prayers answered for the amount needed first, instead of forging ahead, and then looking for the money that does not come in. If God can provide for our needs after, He can just as easily do so before. George Muller spent only what God gave him. He prayed first for the money necessary and waited for God to answer that prayer before going ahead. And that is always a safe procedure. We have no right to incur debts for others to pay. Let us get out and keep out. Debt is a disgrace. It is dishonouring to God.

(10) ALLOWANCE SHOULD BE BASED ON NEEDS, NOT WORTH

The best plan is to share and share alike, that is if we have faith enough to keep the pot full; then there will be sufficient for all. It is dangerous to pay big salaries. Most so-called Faith Missions set aside just sufficient to meet the cost of living, and that is a wise plan. It does not put the missionary too high above the native. It does not overburden the church at home. It honours God. Too much equipment is a hindrance rather than a blessing.

(11) OUR OVERHEAD MUST BE KEPT LOW

One of the greatest criticisms of missionary work today is provoked by the amount used for home expenses. I would strongly advise every contributor to find out just what portion of his dollar actually gets to the field, and how much is used for overhead. Surely fifteen per cent should be sufficient to take care of the needs at home, and even that should be so designated. If money is given for the foreign field, to the foreign field it should go.

These, then, are the principles and practices that should govern missionary work. To ignore them is to court disaster. To apply them is to experience the blessing of God.

CHAPTER XVI

ARE NOT THE RELIGIONS OF THE HEATHEN GOOD ENOUGH FOR THEM?

TOURISTS come home and tell us that the heathen are better off as they are, and that their religions are good enough for them. They say they are happy in their heathenism and that it is a mistake to send missionaries to them.

Now the Bible says that "the dark places of the earth are full of the habitations of cruelty" (Ps. 74:20). And so it is. The trouble is, the tourists do not stay long enough to find out. Heathenism is characterized by cruelty. Fear grips their hearts. They are in constant dread of evil spirits, spirits that must somehow be appeased.

AFRICA

I am thinking now of my visit to Africa and the story I was told. It was at midnight. Suddenly there was a death wail in the village; a little baby had died. Immediately the witch doctor was called. The villagers were aroused. Before very long he had pointed out a woman whom he accused of having caused the death of the little one. She immediately protested, insisting that she was innocent, but she had to be tried. They hurried her away to the tree that stood in the centre of the village. She was told to climb it and then hurl herself from the topmost bough. She began to climb. Presently she sat on one of the branches and again protested her innocence. Everyone knew she was telling the truth. She was one of the finest women in the village, highly respected by all, but the witch doctor had pointed her out as the one guilty, hence she had to prove her innocence.

Then she commenced climbing again, until she had reached the very highest limb of the tree. There she sat, again maintaining her innocence. Then, before the horrified gaze of the missionary, she threw herself down to the hard ground and was instantly killed, most of the bones of her body being broken. She was thereby judged guilty. Had she been innocent, she would have been unharmed.

That, my friends, has happened in the case of hundreds upon hundreds. WHY? Because of religion. Heathen religions demand it, hence there is no escape. Would you be willing to take her place? Until you are prepared to accept her religion and give up your Christianity let no one ever hear you say, "Their religions are good enough for them." If they are not good enough for you, then they are not good enough for them.

AUSTRALIA

I am thinking of my visit to the aborigines of Australia. Away back in the heart of that Continent there is an immense desert where it gets very hot, and there the aborigines live, almost naked—oftentimes sleeping on the sand. A mother gives birth to a baby. Someone in the village dies. A victim must be found.

Before long the witch doctor makes his way towards the newborn babe. The mother clutches it frantically to her breast, but without a moment's hesitation the witch doctor tears it from her arms and, amid her shrieks and cries, lays it on its back on the sand, forces open its little mouth, takes handfuls of sand and pours it into the open mouth and down the throat, until its mouth is filled with sand and the little thing strangles to death. WHY? Because their religions demand it. There must be a human sacrifice. Evil spirits have to be appeased.

Would you be willing to change places with that mother? If her religion is good enough for her, then it is good enough for you. But unless you are willing to take her place and have your little new-born baby torn from your arms and put to death, as hers was, you have no right to say that their religions are good enough for them. It is because of religion that these horrible practices are carried on.

Do you not think that the mother suffers, just as you would suffer? Of course she does. She feels for her baby as you would feel for your baby, but the witch doctor knows no mercy; the spirits must be satisfied. Is her religion good enough for her? Then it is good enough for you.

THE SOUTH SEA ISLANDS

I am thinking, too, of my visit to the South Sea Islands. John Geddes was one of the first missionaries to go to the South Sea Islands from Canada. It was years ago now. As he stepped ashore he saw a group of people and on the ground the body of a man. Under a tree he saw a young woman. She was the widow of the man who had died.

Suddenly the natives approached her. She was unresisting. Full well she knew what would happen. They placed a cord around her neck, and then commenced to strangle her to death. John Geddes rushed towards her in an effort to rescue her, but he was rudely pushed away and told to mind his own business and that if he didn't he, too, would lose his life. And there before his horrified eyes he saw that beautiful young woman slowly strangled to death and her body placed beside that of her husband.

WHY? Because their religion demanded that when a husband died his widow must be strangled to death to accompany him on his journey. And if the eldest son is old enough he is the one who must strangle his mother. Moreover, all the children, if they are too young to support themselves, must likewise be put to death. That is religion, heathen religion.

Would you be willing, my friend, to change places with that widow? Could you look forward to such an experience in the event of your husband's death? If their religions are good enough for them, then they are good enough for you; and if they are not good enough for you, then do not say that they are good enough for them.

INDIA

Never will I forget my visit to India. Many a time, as I walked by the side of the river, did my mind go back to that day when the body of the husband was placed on a pile of wood, and then the widow, still alive and well, placed beside him, and the two bodies, one dead and the other alive, bound together, and then the whole set on fire. There, amid the shrieks and screams of the dying widow as she slowly burned to death, the natives gathered around, believing that the evil spirits were being pacified, and that now the husband would have his wife in the other life.

Do you mean to say that you would be willing to change places with that widow? Thousands upon thousands of widows died in the flames when their husbands died, just because of religion. Are their religions good enough for them? Then they must also be good enough for you. If you, my friend, would not be willing to exchange places with that widow, giving up your Christianity and taking her heathen religion, then do not say that their religions are good enough for them and that they are better off as they are. Could a widow be happy enduring such torture? Of course not. "The dark places of the earth are full of the habitations of cruelty."

MOHAMMEDANISM

Will I ever forget the story of that Mohammedan who stood before the people in the centre of the town and hacked his skull with a great, long knife until the blood flowed freely, and then took newspapers and stuck them into those open gashes, after which he deliberately struck a match and set the whole on fire? There he stood, the fire sizzling the blood, burning the paper and the hair; the man enduring the most excruciating agony.

WHY? you ask. Because of his religion. He must afflict his body; he must suffer; he must endure torture in order to gain a place in Heaven, and so he tormented himself. Would you be willing to exchange places with him? Would his religion be good enough for you? Could you endure such torment? Would you be willing to suffer as he suffered? Oh, my friend, unless his religion is good enough for you, do not say that it is good enough for him.

SOUTH-EAST ASIA

Come to South-East Asia. We are among the tribes-people. A helpless little girl is lying on her back, her head firmly held between the knees of an inhuman monster, who with a coarse saw is deliberately sawing her beautiful front teeth off at the gums. The perspiration stands in beads upon her almost naked body as she endures the dreadful pain. Nerves are exposed. Blood pours from her mouth. Pain, indescribable, is endured, until at last the hideous, barbarous operation is over and she is released, to live her life with nothing but ugly gums. Would you change places with her? What about your own little girl? Would you want her to suffer such torture? Yet countless thousands have borne it and all because of a heathen religion, little innocent victims, unable to escape. That is heathenism. If such a religion is good enough for them, it is good enough for you.

The heathen are NOT better off as they are. They are NOT happy, they are miserable. They are most unhappy, they are wretched, they suffer, they are in fear of evil spirits constantly, they are always attempting to appease them. There is no rest in heathenism, no peace, no joy. Only Jesus Christ can impart joy. Therefore let us do everything we possibly can to give them the Gospel before it is forever too late, that they may experience the joy that you and I know in Christ. Let us never again say, "THEY ARE BETTER OFF AS THEY ARE. THEIR RELIGIONS ARE GOOD ENOUGH FOR THEM."

CHAPTER XVII

MISSIONS THROUGH EVANGELISM

EVANGELISTIC campaigns are needed on the foreign field just as much as they are here at home. But in only a few centres have they been held, at least until recently. Something was done in years gone by in South America and Central America as well as on the mission fields of Europe. But for the most part, the missionary societies have not used the method of mass evangelism in their work. I believe that every large city in the foreign field should see an evangelistic campaign. The campaign should be held in one of the main auditoriums of the city, widely advertised and everything done to get the people to attend. As a matter of fact, it is easier to get a large attendance in foreign lands than it is here at home.

PREPARING THE WAY

Paul, you will remember, went everywhere preaching the Gospel and he never seemed to be satisfied until he had an uproar. He went from city to city. If the people were indifferent and unresponsive, he did something that created a disturbance. He knew that if he could get everyone talking about the Gospel, something could be done.

People should either be made mad or glad. As long as they are indifferent, there will be few results. The quickest way to make the Gospel known throughout the entire city is to have an uproar, a disturbance that will get everyone excited and interested, something that the papers will take up and write about. Whether they are in favour or against, whether they write for the Gospel or in opposition to it makes no difference.

The main thing to do is to get them talking until everyone is discussing the issue.

After that, the missionaries can quietly move in and gather up the results. They will meet people who know something about what they are talking about and it will be easier for them to discuss spiritual things and to win souls for Christ. A disturbance is a wonderful asset. There is nothing like an evangelistic campaign to create an uproar.

Let all the churches in every foreign city get together and hold great evangelistic, soul-winning campaigns in the largest auditoriums. Let them join hands. Only then can they advance. A little boy was lost. Hundreds searched in vain. At last they joined hands—1,000 of them—and walked across the fields. Soon he was found, but it was too late; he was dead. They had worked alone too long. Had they united sooner, they could have saved him.

During the autumn of 1957 I held eight great campaigns in South America. In Montevideo seventy-one churches joined hands and held the greatest meetings ever seen in the history of the city. Over 600 came to Christ in one week. Thousands were blessed and helped. The largest hall in the country, with its 8,500 seats, was taken. In Buenos Aires 300 churches co-operated in a place holding 25,000. It was packed to capacity and over 1,500 accepted Christ. It was the same in Sao Paulo, Curitiba, Rosario, Santiago and Lima. As many as 6,000 crowded into a building seating less than 4,000. Hundreds thronged the inquiry rooms. In the eight campaigns there were some 10,000 decisions, 4,500 of them first-time decisions for salvation.

EXTENDING THE INVITATION

A number of years ago, I was travelling through what was then called the Dutch East Indies. I was asked to hold an evangelistic campaign in a tabernacle that had been recently built in one of the larger cities. I did so.

Night after night, I preached the Gospel of the Lord Jesus

Christ, preached it to Buddhists, Mohammedans and those of other religions. The auditorium was packed to capacity. Even the head-hunters from Borneo were there, many of them. It was a great joy to proclaim the Gospel message.

Toward the middle of the campaign, I felt that the time had come to extend an invitation and so I went to the missionaries and told them that I was going to invite lost men and women to accept Jesus Christ that night, and I urged them to be ready to do personal work. They looked at me in amazement. At first I could not understand it.

"Why," I asked, "what's the matter? Don't you want me to give an invitation?" "No," they replied. "As a matter of fact you can't give an invitation here." "I can't!" I responded. "Why not?" "Well, it isn't done, we just don't do it that way." "Why not?" I persisted. "Why shouldn't I extend the invitation?" "Oh," they answered, "people would lose face. If you were to give an invitation and no one should come, it would be dangerous; we would not be able to confront the people again."

"How then, do you win souls?" I inquired. "Oh," they said, "we just go on preaching and sowing the seed." "Then," I continued, "what happens?" "Well," they said, "finally someone gets convicted and at last comes to inquire the way of salvation. We explain it and endeavour to lead him to Christ." "How many come?" I asked. "Not very many. We cannot quite understand it. We get a few, but only a few. However, we know of no other way to get results."

"Well," I said, "I am going to give an invitation. I've travelled all over the Russian mission fields of Europe. Everywhere I've gone, I've held campaigns in the larger cities and have extended the invitation. I've travelled all over Spain and I've done the very same thing there. I have travelled all through Germany, France, Poland and many other countries, conducting evangelistic meetings. Everywhere I've gone, I have invited men and women to come to the Lord Jesus Christ. If it has worked in their fields, then it will work here. And so tonight, I am going to give the invitation."

Again they remonstrated. "It would be impossible," they said. "It just could not be done here. Oriental people are different. There would be no response." "Well," I said, "let me try. Let us see what God will do. He can see us through." At last, with many misgivings, they agreed.

That night, when I had concluded my message, I immediately gave an invitation. "All those," I said, "who would like to be saved tonight, please raise your hand." Immediately about fifty hands were raised. "Now, will all those who raised their hands, kindly stand?" There was not a movement. No one budged. Not a single individual stood. I could not understand it. I thought that perhaps they had misunderstood me and so again I made the same request: "Will all those who raised their hands, kindly stand?" Once again there was perfect silence. Not an individual moved.

Suddenly dear David Clench, who had been sitting on the platform back of me, sprang to his feet and coming forward, he put his hand upon the shoulder of my interpreter and pushed him aside. "Now, Dr. Smith," he said, "go on and give your invitation." Not understanding, I turned once more to the audience and again asked my question.

In a moment about forty individuals stood to their feet. Then I continued my invitation. "Will those who are standing," I asked, "kindly come forward and kneel here at the front?" Without a moment's hesitation, they moved to the front, fell down upon their knees and started to pour out their hearts to God.

Later on, I asked for an explanation from the missionary who had intervened. He told me that my interpreter, afraid of losing face, instead of interpreting my request, "Will all those who have raised their hands kindly stand?", changed it completely and interpreted it, "Will all those who have raised their hands, kindly remain seated?" He, like the missionaries, had feared for the results. But when the young missionary gave the invitation as I had given it, there was an immediate response.

I was just about to explain to them the way of salvation

more perfectly when they started to confess their sins and pray aloud. Within about twenty or thirty minutes, most of them had made decisions for the Lord Jesus Christ and were standing before me with shining faces, rejoicing in the Saviour. It was a wonderful night. No one who was present will ever forget it.

Months later, after I returned to Canada, the leader, Rev. Robert A. Jaffray, wrote me and stated that they were still giving the invitation, the Spirit of revival was still upon them, and God was still working in their midst and saving souls.

I believe that any man who is called to be an evangelist here in America can also be an evangelist in the foreign fields of earth. It is my conviction that every great city on the foreign field ought to have an evangelistic campaign. I would like to see evangelists go from city to city throughout the entire world and put on exactly the same kind of campaign that we put on here in the homeland. It could speed up the evangelization of the world.

CHAPTER XVIII

OUR MISSIONARY MOTTOES

"YOU MUST go or send a substitute."—*Oswald J. Smith.*
"This generation can only reach this generation."
"The mission of the Church is missions."
"Anywhere, provided it be forward."—*David Livingstone.*
"Farther, still farther, into the night."
"If God wills the evangelization of the world, and you refuse to support missions, then you are opposed to the will of God."—*Oswald J. Smith.*
"Attempt great things for God, expect great things from God."—*Wm. Carey.*
"The church that does not evangelize will fossilize."
"Why should anyone hear the Gospel twice before everyone has heard it once."—*Oswald J. Smith.*
"You can't take it with you, but you can send it on ahead."
—*Oswald J. Smith.*
"Only as the Church fulfils her missionary obligation does she justify her existence."
"A man may die leaving upwards of a million, without taking any of it upwards."—*Wm. Fetler.*
"The light that shines farthest shines brightest nearest home."
"If Jesus Christ be God and died for me, then no sacrifice can be too great for me to make for Him."—*C.T. Studd.*
"Give according to your income lest God make your income according to your giving."—*Peter Marshall.*
"The prospects are as bright as the promises of God."
—*Judson.*
"Now let me burn out for God."—*Henry Martyn.*
"Yet more, O my God, more toil, more agony, more suffering for Thee."—*Francis Xavier.*

"We can give without loving, but we cannot love without giving."

"The church which ceases to be evangelistic will soon cease to be evangelical."—*Alexander Duff.*

"Not, how much of *my* money will I give to God, but, how much of God's money will I keep for myself?"

"The supreme task of the Church is the evangelization of the world."

"Untold millions are still untold."

"You have one business on earth—to save souls."—*John Wesley.*

"Sympathy is no substitute for action."

"Christ alone can save the world, but Christ cannot save the world alone."

"The best remedy for a sick church is to put it on a missionary diet."

"If we have not enough in our religion to drive us to share it with all the world, it is doomed here at home."

"Do we pray 'Thy kingdom come', but never say, 'Here am I, Lord, send me?'"

"God had an only Son and He made Him a missionary." — *David Livingstone.*

"As long as there are millions destitute of the Word of God and knowledge of Jesus Christ, it will be impossible for me to devote my time and energy to those who have both."—*J. L. Ewen.*

"The first work of the whole Church is to give the Gospel to the whole world."

"Why should so few hear the Gospel again and again when so many have never heard it once?"—*Oswald J. Smith.*

"I am destined to proclaim the message, unmindful of personal consequences to myself."—*Zinzendorf.*

"I declare, now I am dying, I would not have spent my life otherwise for the whole world."—*David Brainerd.*

"I cared not where or how I lived, or what hardships I went through, so that I could but gain souls to Christ."—*David Brainerd.*

"Square with God and God will square with you."—*Oswald J. Smith.*

"You can't beat God giving."—*Oswald J. Smith.*

"God will be no man's debtor."—*Oswald J. Smith.*

"I have seen the Vision and for self I cannot live;
Life is less than worthless till my all I give."
                              —*Oswald J. Smith.*